ZEN AND REALITY

ZEN
AND REALITY

An Approach to Sanity and Happiness on a Non-Sectarian Basis

ROBERT POWELL

THE VIKING PRESS   NEW YORK

LIBRARY OF CONGRESS CATALOGING IN PUBLICATION DATA
Powell, Robert.
    Zen and reality.
    Reprint of the 1961 ed. published by Allen and Unwin,
London.
    Bibliography: p.
    1. Zen Buddhism. I. Title.
BQ9265.6.P68   1974   294.3'927   74-5808
ISBN: 0-670-00588-6

Printed in U.S.A.

*Acknowledgment is made to the following for permission to quote
from the sources indicated.*

GEORGES BORCHARDT, INC.: From *Buddha and Buddhism* by
Maurice Percheron, translated by Edmund Stapleton.

THE FIRST ZEN INSTITUTE OF AMERICA, INC.: From *The Development of Chinese Zen after the Sixth Patriarch,* by H. Doumoulin
and R. F. Sasaki.

ARTHUR GUIRDAM: From *A Theory of Disease,* by Arthur
Guirdam.

HARPER & ROW, PUBLISHERS, INC.: From *The First and Last
Freedom,* by J. Krishnamurti.

HUTCHINSON PUBLISHING GROUP LTD.: From *Essays in Zen Buddhism,* by D. T. Suzuki, vol. 2

PANTHEON BOOKS, INC., A DIVISION OF RANDOM HOUSE, INC.:
From *The Way of Zen,* by Alan W. Watts, Copyright © 1957 by
Pantheon Books, Inc. From *The Supreme Identity,* by Alan W.
Watts, published in 1950. Reprinted by permission.

VEDANTA PRESS: From *The Song of God: Bhagavad-Gita,* translated by Swami Prabhavananda and Christopher Isherwood.

CONTENTS

PART ONE

I

KRISHNAMURTI AND ZEN

Krishnamurti is one of the few men who became a legend in their own lifetime. He owes this to a number of factors, least of all probably to the publishing of some books as far as the public are concerned. Yet it is these scarce writings alone that are sufficient evidence to stamp him as the most creative mind of our time, for what Krishnamurti has done in the psychological sphere may well be compared to the revolution in physics effected by Einstein. The latter's theory of relativity took as its point of departure the simple fact that the speed of light is observed to be a constant under all circumstances, independent of movement from or toward the light source. Krishnamurti's point of departure was the equally simple observation that all psychological suffering begins and ends in and through the mind: 'The mind is its own prison'. Therefore, transformation, liberation from suffering can only be achieved by the ending of the ceaseless activity of the mind.

Krishnamurti's message—if one may call it that—is really that *life itself* is pleasurable (although this word is used here in a very special sense); but, that we do not know, have never even sensed this happiness because we are constantly tied up in the process of seeking gratification by becoming something, achieving some result—which is the uncreative process of time. Uncreative, because it is based on memory, on recognizing that which is experience, that which is the past. All his recorded lectures have been concerned in pointing out —and in every talk this is effected from a different angle— this unproductive process of the mind, which has to come to a stop before truth can be uncovered.

In actual fact, what his message implies is that it is possible to add as it were another dimension to one's being—or more accurately, re-discover, realize this extra dimension in which we have always been living but did not know it. When we have had this realization, the timeless, the eternal has come into being and truth comes to us. Truth, which is inexpressible and unthinkable, because the moment it is expressed and thought about—in other words, named, classified and verbalized—it is no longer truth but a secondary thing of space and time. It is essential, therefore, to see that such realization is more in the nature of an opening up, a clearing away of impediments, of that which is in time—that truth has always been with us and yet does not belong to you or me; in fact, it is the centre of the 'me' which—through its incessant activities—has prevented me from realizing.

We can now see that there is no path towards reality, truth, and hence that no *guru* can lead us. A *guru* can only lead you from the known to the known—and for the known to come to an end only your own being is involved. For the mind, which is the known, and the product of the past, of time, to dissolve is the very opposite process. It means the cessation of all seeking, all thought, all the mind's activities in the nature of clinging or grasping directed at self-assertion or spiritual gain. This happens—not by discipline, not by repression, not by choice—but spontaneously once the mind has understood the nature of its own activities, realized its own futility. When the mind sees that its inherent sickness is itself, it quietens, it shuts up—suddenly and without any forewarning or intimation. Thus, uninvited, that which is not of the mind, not of time, that which is real comes into being—not by a process of becoming, but by being what *is*.

Although the author feels that Krishnamurti cannot be compared with any other religious thinker or philosopher, many readers may want to enquire how his teaching fits in with that of other great teachers. Let us first recognize that Krishnamurti's approach is original and based on his own direct experience, although the gist of it may be similar or even partly identical with what others have proclaimed before him. It is a way of liberation, not a teaching in the actual sense of the word. Being primarily a plea for self-help (there being no alternative), his 'philosophy' becomes entirely intelligible only in the process of self-discovery.

The question which we are naturally asking ourselves is: Does any other teaching exist which is in bare essentials similar or identical to Krishnamurti's? The answer must be yes; for there is such a teaching in Zen, the Japanese form of Buddhism, which has developed from a cross of Taoism* and the Mahayana School of Buddhism. Furthermore, Krishnamurti's notion of 'awareness' finds its counterpart in Bare Attention or Mindfulness—also called Satipatthana. However, it is Krishnamurti's great merit to have more strongly emphasized than anyone the essential requirement of passivity: the awareness must be completely without any form of evaluation to be of value; otherwise it becomes merely another technique of introspection or self-analysis.

Returning now to Zen, let us look into the allegation of some people that Zen is just another 'ism', another system of knowledge—and, therefore, far removed from the spirit of Krishnamurti. Let us see if this is correct by examining some 'definitions' and quotations which seem typical of the spirit of Zen from some of its prominent exponents:—

'Outside teaching; apart from tradition
Not founded on words and letters.
Pointing directly to the human mind
Seeing into one's nature and attaining Buddhahood'.[1]

'There is no place in Buddhism for using effort. Just be ordinary and nothing special. Relieve your bowels, pass water, put on your clothes, and eat your food. When you're tired, go and lie down. Ignorant people may laugh at me, but the wise will understand.'—Lin-chi.[2]

'If you students of the Way do not awake to this Mind substance, you will overlay Mind with conceptual thought, you will seek the Buddha outside yourselves, and you will remain attached to forms, pious practices and so on, all of which are harmful and not at all the way to supreme knowledge.'—Huang-Po.[3]

* Chinese Way of Liberation, supposedly first clearly propounded by Lao-tse. His teaching was subsequently disseminated and elaborated by Chuang-tzu, some of whose utterances appear on p. 43.

And finally, from the same Master:—

'By their very seeking they lose it, for that is using the Buddha to seek for the Buddha and using mind to grasp Mind. Even though they do their utmost for a full aeon, they will not be able to attain it.'[4]

It seems to me that if we really get down to the heart of these quotations and are not frightened by the Buddhist 'jargon' used, we shall find that Krishnamurti and Zen are in essence the same thing, the same teaching. although using different modes of expression. Both are not 'teachings' in the accepted sense of the word but pointers to an immediate transformation of man ('attaining Buddhahood') which is only possible through complete self-knowledge ('seeing into one's own nature'), and not through the following of systems, doctrines, or practising asceticism or disciplines of any kind.

[1] A. W. Watts, *The Way of Zen*, London, Thames & Hudson, 1957, p. 88.
[2] *Ibid.*, p. 101.
[3] J. Blofield, *The Zen Teaching of Huang Po on the Transmission of Mind*, London, Rider, 1958, p. 31.
[4] *Ibid.*, p. 29.

WHAT CAN WE DO? (1)

Krishnamurti states that we cannot learn wisdom from books or teachers. In other words, we must ask ourselves the question: Can an idea (even if this idea is based on someone else's experience of truth) cause transformation? Does knowing the cause of suffering stop suffering? We can see all around us that this is not so. The drug addict knows very well the cause of his suffering; yet he cannot put an end to his misery. Merely knowing the Buddha's Four Noble Truths, or learning the Holy Scriptures by heart, does not change us. It does not release us from bondage but it may in fact add a fresh bond to our shackles: that of trying to live up to a formula, an idea. It is because of these obvious facts that Krishnamurti says that the person who verbally repeats a truth, is stating a lie. The crux of the matter is that an experience of truth can never be conveyed to another person: it is private. When for instance, someone talks about having experienced the Oneness of things, the experience itself was neither of the One nor the Many but transcended both. Hence the inability of the experiencer to express himself in words, for the Word always represents one term of a pair of opposites, whereas experience lies beyond the verbal level, where the opposites are transcended. Any statement about a spiritual experience is therefore merely a figure of speech which cannot really teach anyone anything.

Now what happens when we abandon *all* ideas about truth, life; if we realize that the so-called acceptance of an abstract principle (even if that principle is a logically correct statement) can not produce a fundamental change because it does not break up the deeply rooted habitual processes that make up the life of the self? Aren't we then open and alert to receive truth, to experiencing afresh what is from moment to moment without the intervening action of 'idea', that only seeks to fit each experience into a pattern of its own—a pattern that is always of the past, of the known? Isn't the unknown constantly being reduced to the known, without giving up any of its significance? Isn't the living experience of the now, which is always fresh, always different from any previous experience—continuously being translated into terms of the old?

But living without idea means living without residue from the past—it means experiencing and dying continually to the experience. The 'me', which is psychological memory, the sum total of all my possessions, ideas, beliefs, hopes, fears, etc. which is retained in 'my' consciousness—is then no longer being nourished by experience.

Once I start observing in my everyday activities how everything I do is habitual, i.e. it is a reaction of my mind, which is conditioned by the past, to the challenge of the present—a process that gives continued life to these stored-up ideas and emotions—this process weakens and loses its hold. The ego relaxes when it recognizes it is the past struggling against the present. Finally there will be a state of pure experiencing in which the 'me' is not. Paradoxically enough: the fully integrated personality is that of the man who is no longer conscious of having a personality.

The weakening of the ego must however be understood not as the result of any action of the ego itself—for this would imply a contradiction—but as the result of Intelligence, or Truth if you like, which transcends the limits of the individual. The situation may therefore be summed up paradoxically as follows: As long as I cling to any idea, method or any other form of activity to progress towards enlightenment, I am slipping back. Only if I really see that I cannot do anything, why I cannot do anything, and I then no longer wish to do anything—only then might something happen, not a progressive change, but a sudden one. The following quotation from Alan Watts appears relevant: 'In short, then, there is no action whereby the ego can, of itself, produce or attain realization. As Shankara insists again and again, realization is the fruit of knowledge, not of action; it is the dissolution of nescience (*avidya*) or unconsciousness, and as darkness is not thrust aside by waving one's arms but only by the appearance of light, so nescience is overcome by knowing* and not doing. Thus he argues that if action could produce realization, a realization so attained would not be eternal.'

Curiously enough, this attitude of passivity one finds emphasized in many different kinds of religious writings: in Taoism this is 'wu-wei' (which can be roughly translated as 'non-interference'), in Zen it is called 'let-go' and 'obedience to the nature of things', in Christianity 'surrendering to the Will of God', and in Krishnamurti, 'awareness'.

Now what exactly is meant by 'awareness'? Is it not in some way different from passivity? It is this: doing absolutely nothing; it becomes a reality when the mind has become quite still. It can not therefore be called a practice. Normally we 'do' all the time and it is through this doing that we never completely understand anything. This is so even when we think we do absolutely nothing: there is the continuous activation by our desires, emotions, etc.—in short, the so-called 'emotional-imaginative film' (cf., H. Benoit, *The Supreme Doctrine*) that unrolls itself before our mind's eye. It is like listening in to a Beethoven symphony in a room full of cackling people. Unless they shut up we do not properly take in the music.

Much the same happens in the absence of awareness, when through the interminable chatter of our minds we cannot properly observe and take in our experience. The experience is constantly acted upon by the mind in order to be changed, without ever allowing the experience to give up its own significance—the significance of what *is*. The tragic part is that we are so used to 'doing' that we do not notice it any longer, and then the non-doing—the reversal of our habitual attitude—can only be interpreted as just another form of doing, a 'practice'. Or it is believed that this new state of non-doing can only be brought about by means of some enormous effort, for it is not realized that in this case the means are not different from the end and that it only comes to us when in our attitude towards life there is a radical break with the process of becoming.

---

* 'Knowing' is here to be understood not in the ordinary sense of the word, but rather as 'experiencing', of having a profound insight that goes beyond the intellectual level.

Living a life of wu-wei, of alert passivity, brings mental tranquillity and brings us closer to that condition where 'obedience to the nature of things' is lived without conscious awareness of it. One has become a spectator,* an observer, instead of an actor until such a time that the problem of action is understood once and for all. Because the real basis of Nature is wu-wei, the vegetative existence of the animal kingdom may blossom out in Homo Sapiens to the spiritual life, which is living supremely in tune with Nature. But we don't want to see it that way: we are no longer satisfied with just living which we call 'merely existing' and so we invent living with a capital L—which is improving on Nature by superimposing on it a continuous search for more excitement, more pleasure, as well as more security. And we are so used to all this that we do not even see the futility of it, and apart from that: facing the futility of it would of course mean facing Death from which we try to run away all our lives. Nor do we realize that it is exactly this feverish drive for security that is causing the insecurity and fear which constitute the underlying neurosis of modern man.

A word may be usefully said here about whether wu-wei, passive awareness, is the same as 'quietism'—not because it is an issue but because this question seems to worry many Buddhists and others, and 'quietism' has almost become a dirty word to them. If quietism is understood as fatalism, as Not-Caring, the opposite of intelligence, as non-doing and non-understanding—which means Sleep—then the answer is most certainly no; for wu-wei implies a heightened state of awareness: a maximum of understanding with a minimum of doing. If, on the other hand, quietism is thought of as the cessation of all seeking for achievement, the end of all ambition for gain whether material or spiritual (which is extremely arduous, requiring continuous watchfulness and great intelligence) then the answer is certainly yes—then wu-wei is quietism.

A similar issue, related to the foregoing, is the choice between free will and determinism—for one hears people

---

* See the similarity with the statement attributed to Christ: 'Be a passer-by', a tremendous saying that sums up this whole philosophy of wu-wei (*Secret Sayings of Jesus according to the Gospel of Thomas,* Fontana Books, 1960).

argue as follows: 'If all is determined, why should I bother about self-realization, or about anything else for that matter?'

For the person who really understands, the choice between free will and determinism is resolved. He realizes that for the ordinary person, when he thinks he is acting 'freely', his actions are determined by causes which are obscure to him, because he is not aware of them: in other words, when he thinks he is 'acting' he is merely 'reacting' to exterior contacts. And the person who says 'Why should I bother' as well as the person who can not help himself in his eagerness to find out truth for himself—both have come to their present attitudes through long sequences of cause-and-effects. Therefore, there is no conflict between free will and determinism: the apparent opposition between individual effort and determinism is an illusion based on another illusion—that of the separate self.

As long as there is an individual 'I', the phrase 'free will' is a contradiction in terms, for 'will' can never be free, being simply another word for volition, or desire, which is always based on idea. The point that should interest Buddhists most is that as long as there is an 'I', a decision is based on an idea, and such action is bound to the past, therefore determined. Only when the ego has dissolved is there pure action, i.e. action which is not the result of idea; only then is the chain of cause-and-effects broken, and determinism has come to the end of its tether. In this state when there is only action, without the actor, that action is timeless; and there is a freedom, which is total and absolute, not conditioned in any way because it is free from the net of time.

The illusion of choice occurred because we made the mistake of considering the mind which looks upon these things as standing outside the process of cause and effect—as a separate, unchanging, purely observing entity not influenced by the world process; in other words, by the illusion of the isolated 'I'. In actual fact, the mind is memory at any level, and as such entirely the product of the past, of conditioning —and therefore wholly determined. The Taoist would say: 'All is the Tao and you cannot put yourself outside the Tao— if you go against the Tao it is only apparently so.'

People who do not understand this problem often mistake Buddhism for fatalism. But it must be clear from the foregoing that Buddhism is the very opposite of fatalism. The attitude of the fatalist is somewhat like a miracle worker. He separates fate from the individual and his actions—whereas Buddhists state that the individual's fate is the result of his thought and action. Therefore, to sit back and say: 'I shan't bother—if I am destined for enlightenment I shall attain it anyway regardless how much or how little I understand at present' is to delude oneself. This unrealistic attitude denies causality and implies that there is an entity outside ourselves, which bestows a certain quantum of fate—called 'our destiny'—on each individual. It completely denies the empirical truth that to receive enlightenment one should be ready for it—and that this comes only as the result of intelligence and awareness.

Seeing all this clearly, I now realize that to make a serious effort towards realizing myself is not at all incompatible with the knowledge that 'all is determined'. The latter knowledge does not discourage me by one iota in my undertaking; in fact, I clearly see that it is a completely irrelevant issue to my quest. I am fully aware also that the whole ridiculous free-will/determinism controversy, which has pained thinkers for thousands of years, has been 'manufactured' by these very same philosophers; it has come about through the befuddling effect of words and by the inability of philosophers and intellectuals generally to transcend pairs of opposites. The only important thing and the moral in all this is to realize the futility of quibbling about words, the irrelevancy of making issues out of the labelling of ideas without being able to penetrate beyond the verbal level. Let us leave this childish activity to the professional philosophers and the politicians—for them it represents a livelihood, for us a distraction and a hindrance.

3

WHAT CAN WE DO? (2)

or

HOW TO GAIN A LIFE OF WU-WEI

Firstly, we must see clearly that all this business of working on oneself, spiritual exercises and practices, etc., is also a hindrance in the sense that it implies a change of oneself, i.e. it blinds us to the fact that Nirvana is not a state to be *achieved*, since from the beginning we have been in Nirvana, for Samsara is Nirvana.* It is a state to be *discovered*—and this discovery comes through the understanding of oneself, through passive awareness, and not through the changing or improving of it (that is, if such a progressive 'improvement' is possible at all). The famous Zen master Bankei taught:—'You are primarily Buddhas; you are not going to be Buddhas for the first time. There is not an iota of a thing to be called error in your inborn mind . . . If you have the least desire to be better than you actually are, if you hurry up to the slightest degree in search of something, you are already going against the Unborn'.**

So, when the question comes up: What have we got to do? the answer can only be: *Nothing*. And this is, to my mind, the most wonderful aspect of it: this thing we are talking about is not to be possessed by a few initiates, by the privileged in wealth or in learning—it is open to everyone. It does not require concentration, effort, will power, dis-

---

* 'There is no Nirvana except where is Samsara; there is no Samsara except where is Nirvana; for the condition of existence is not of a mutually exclusive character. Therefore it is said that all things are non-dual as are Nirvana and Samsara.' (D. T. Suzuki, *The Lankavatara Sutra*, London, Routledge, 1932, reprinted 1956, p. 67.)
** D. T. Suzuki, *Living by Zen*, p. 177-78.

ciplines of any sort. It exists here and now, it requires only one thing to see it: openness, freedom—the freedom to be open and not tethered by any ideas, concepts, etc. We can go on reading, studying, attending lectures, etc., until we are blue in the face, all this will not be of the slightest avail —*it is only when we stop thinking and let go, that we can start seeing, discovering.*

When our mind is tranquil, there will be an occasional pause to its feverish activities, there will be a let-go, and it is only then, in the interval between two thoughts, that a flash of understanding—understanding, which is not thought —can take place.

So, the first requirement really is to have a tranquil mind. But as soon as we put it this way and are not extremely careful, we may be tempted to ask ourselves, *how* to get a tranquil mind—and create an additional problem, viz. how to change, what we are, not tranquil, into what we should be or want to be, tranquil—and once again we are caught up in the process of desire, of becoming, creating more conflict and more restlessness.

So, what do we do? Here again, we do nothing, for any doing will prove our undoing, spiritually. We are just passively aware of the situation we are finding ourselves in without condemnation, without wanting to escape from it; and purely observe because we are intensely interested and want to find out: we are watching with the same keen interest with which a scientist is observing a newly discovered phenomenon of nature.

When we thus watch the movements of a restless mind and see that by itself it is incapable of setting itself free— Bankei compared this vain effort at liberation with washing off blood with blood—when we go through it with complete understanding, which means not merely intellectually (which after all is only on the level of words), but stay with this restlessness and experience it to the full without naming it, at last the experiencer and the experience of restlessness will merge to become one.

Then see if this process (which is true meditation) has not a liberating effect, resulting in peace and tranquillity; the relaxation that follows upon the discovery that one has been chasing one's own shadow, that from the beginning there was nothing that restrained us: that it was merely the illusion of a separate entity, the experiencer, that had to undergo restraint. It is instructive in this connection to recount once again the now famous interview of Tao-hsin (579-651), the Fourth Patriarch, with his predecessor Seng-ts'an. When Tao-hsin came to Seng-ts'an he asked:—

'What is the method of liberation?'
'Who binds you?' replied Seng-ts'an.
'No one binds me.'
'Why then,' asked Seng-ts'an, 'should you seek liberation?'*

At this moment Tao-hsin had his satori.

Let us finally approach this question of doing or non-doing from a slightly different angle. When I think of doing anything at all, of working upon myself in order to improve, then this logically entails dualistic thinking: I have created an entity to be improved, an ego. This ego represents a picture, an idea, which I hold of myself: an abstraction of what I was (representing selected features of my life to date) and never of what 'I' am now. Therefore, self-improvement binds me to the past, to time; it strengthens the separation between thinker and thought, and deepens the illusion of being under restraint. Paradoxically, I can only free myself when I realize that essentially I am free and that therefore there is nothing to be done about it. This comes about immediately I break with the past and step out of time, that is, when I live wholly in the present. For then, there is no longer any psychological memory that gives me continuity as an ego—there is only pure experiencing without the experiencer. This is absolute freedom for there is no longer anything to be liberated, nor has anything been liberated.

So we see, that really the only thing that is required is to forget the past; this also implies that all looking forward ceases. This does not, of course, mean that I should start suffering from general amnesia and forget my knowledge about the world, my job, etc., but it does mean that I should 'lose' that whole bundle of memories of ideas, experiences, etc., that together give me the 'build-up' of being the par-

* A. W. Watts, The Way of Zen, p. 89.

ticular person I am, the feeling of being an 'I'. It signifies particularly that I should let go of all knowledge which up to now has given me a feeling of security. Now it is important to realize that forgetting comes about, not when we try to forget (for this again would imply the dualism of the forgetter and that which he wants to forget), but only when thought comes to an end spontaneously and naturally. Thought, which is the response of memory, arises only when an experience has not been completely understood, and therefore leaves a residue (Buddhists call this residue 'karma'); it ends only when it is completed, thought out, felt out to its fullest extent. Then the residue is done away with and there is the peace of pure being, without past or future.

4

THE TWO WAYS OF LIFE

The natural man† lives entirely for and in his imagination.* All his strivings, all his objectives are constructs of his mind which is for ever in agitation. Since he identifies himself with the imagination and thinks he is nothing more, he is urged on continuously by a chain of self-imposed tasks with their resultant petty satisfactions and frustrations. Not knowing the origin of the imaginative-emotive film which develops itself before his mind's eye he never has a moment's repose. Tossed hither and thither, like a fallen leaf in the autumn wind, he moves from desire to desire without let-up, without ever experiencing complete tranquillity. Hence we read in the Bhagavad-Gita:—**

> The uncontrolled mind
> Does not guess that the Atman*** is present:
> How can it meditate?
> Without meditation, where is peace?
> Without peace, where is happiness?

As the imagination feeds partly on external, and partly on internal stimuli, it looks to the subject deceptively as though he is basing his life firmly on the solid ground of experience, of Reality. Not being aware that these desires, these self-imposed objectives are figments of his imagination and that

† By 'natural' man is designated man before satori.
* Throughout this essay a sharp distinction is maintained between the terms 'imagination', signifying here egotistical activity, and 'inspiration', 'love', etc., meaning constructive, creative activity.
** This and the following excerpts are from the translation by C. Isherwood and Swami Prabhavananda, *The Song of God: Bhagavad Gita*, London, Phoenix House, 1956.
*** It is possible to make this term the subject of a theological controversy, but the author of the present work takes it to mean the same as 'the You which is Not You' (see p. 66). (See also quotation on p. 100.)

they spring ultimately from an urge for self-assertion, which is caused by ignorance about the self (the fear of negation, death), he has no inkling that there are different levels of Reality; and that the man who is unable to contact the deeper, impersonal levels of reality lives a lie, lives in a dream world of his own making. In the Gita the Lord Krishna sums up the situation for Arjuna as follows: 'All living creatures are led astray as soon as they are born, by the delusion that this relative world is real.' In fact, it may be said that the only difference between the average natural man and the man who is given to daydreaming is one of degree; the latter is merely an extreme case of the former.

Educated in the philosophy of 'getting the most out of life', and not simply how to live, modern man never pauses to reflect whether it is thus possible to separate himself from the main stream of life. He is madly obsessed with the idea of 'getting on' but never questions towards what he is getting on. Towards death perhaps? Yet logically, that would be his only answer, for if one thing is absolutely certain it is this, that from the moment he is born he is progressing towards this final and inevitable state. But this inconvenient fact is pushed back as far as possible from his conscious mind, for it is inconsistent with his materialistic philosophy and with his outlook of living for the future but never in the present. Consequently he carries on foolishly with all the useless activities of gathering material and other kinds of possessions to himself as though he had life immortal—at the same time that subconsciously the repressed idea of death is working through in him to give rise to an ever stronger fear of death with the innumerable other fears that all spring from the fear of final and total negation.

Physically the state of mind of the natural man is well expressed by his inability to relax, to sit down and do entirely nothing for even a short time. So firmly has his mind been cultivated to nourish itself on one experience after another, that immediately there is a lull, he has to seek for new stimuli from the outside world. Especially for Western man it can be said that his greatest problem is how to un-tense his mind and bring its ceaseless activities to a stop. For only then can man discover he is something more than his imagination and not a mere machine that reacts mechanically to outside stimuli. Only thus can he find out that another, more real life is possible, is, in fact, his birthright.

Few people have experienced this other life or even have an inkling that such a life is possible. Their present way of life is not so much a conviction with them as a habit, and the breaking of any habit is always painful—and even more so when the habit is lifelong.

However, sometimes when there is a strong urge to know, to find out the real nature of one's self and to understand completely the process of one's own thought, there is a break-through, as it were, an intellectual illumination that does not fail to have repercussions throughout all one's activities; in fact, a transformation of one's habits may take place as a result of the insights acquired.* The Gita states in this connection: 'Even if you are the most sinful of sinners, this insight will carry you like a raft above all your sin.' (Where the word 'sin' is used in Eastern writings it never has the same connotation as in Christian terminology; it is more to be conceived as blind ignorance). It will then be discovered that we are more than this superficial activity of self-expansion, that—as Hubert Benoit put it in *The Supreme Doctrine* —there is something in us that works darkly in our favour. When we experience this fact as a truth, we recognize that what sustains us is a more real, a more fundamental life than the activities of our consciousness.

To come to such a revolutionary insight, however, the complete understanding and realization of 'the Void' is a prerequisite—in fact, it appears to be the only way through which enlightenment can come. Sunya (Sanskrit for 'void') is a term used by Nagarjuna to describe the nature of reality, or rather, of the ideas which man can have about reality. But, of course, if we are consistent, then even the idea of 'Sunya' itself is void; therefore:—

---

* Colin Wilson writes in *The Outsider*, London, Gollancz, 1956 (p. 195): 'Life is such a tissue of delusions that man can never have the remotest idea of who he is or what he is doing—but this dream of unreality can suddenly break (given the right conditions) and the resulting glimpse is a flash of sudden complete understanding. Even if this does not last life can never be the same after this.'

It cannot be called void or not void,
Or both or neither;
But in order to point it out,
It is called 'the Void'.

(Madhyamika Shastra, XV, 3)

Realizing this fully, however, entails much more than a mere intellectual acceptance of the dialectic of Sunyavada as this comes to us in the writings of Nagarjuna. It requires the discovery by oneself of the unreality, the relativity of all verbal assertions, concepts and ideas, including the concept of one's own 'ego'.

The basic cause of why man remains unaware of the Void is that he thinks verbally, that is, he uses words as symbols for reality and he manipulates these symbols as levers for his thoughts—yet he does not understand the real underlying nature of the symbols. He is like a craftsman with only imperfect knowledge of his tools. Krishnamurti has stated in this connection: 'So long as I am ignorant of myself, so long as I am unaware of the total process of myself, I have no basis for thought, for action. But for most of us, that is the last we want: to know ourselves.'

In recent years a close examination of words used in philosophical discourse has been carried out and this has given rise to a new branch of philosophy called 'semantics' or 'meta-linguistics'. All this is very useful but only on its own level. For after all words, being abstractions, when further defined by other abstractions, still remain on the relative plane. Complete understanding and insight of an 'object' is therefore always acquired before it is named. (This understanding of the 'thing' in its totality is called 'prajna' or higher intuition in Buddhist terminology). It must now also be clear that words, concepts and ideas by themselves, can only give rise to systems representing relationships of abstractions or symbols, and these can never lead to liberation. In other words, no philosophy can transcend duality, can embrace the Absolute: that which is not of time and space. Man can only experience Reality when he has emptied himself of all concepts, ideas, and symbols of any kind.

So we see that understanding the Void implies somewhat more than a realization of the simple adage: 'All the world's a stage', which, although it expresses the feeling that the drama of existence is predetermined, appears still conceived dualistically. Here again Krishnamurti may be usefully quoted: 'Revolution, this psychological, creative revolution, in which the "me" is not, comes only when the thinker and thought are one, when there is no duality such as the thinker controlling thought; and I suggest it is this experience alone that releases the creative energy which in turn brings about a fundamental revolution, the breaking up of the psychological "me".'*

In general, it may be said that in order to live this way completely—in other words, free ourselves from the stranglehold of the imagination, which originally has created the idea of the 'me' and which cannot do anything else but protect and bolster up this ego—it is essential never to lose touch with the Void. This is achieved when we are mindful of every thought, every emotion and every image that comes to our mind. When we fully realize the relativity and origin of each such experience, we have put our life, so to say, within a framework of reference, that is Absolute instead of merely Personal. By persisting in this inner 'work' we are basing our life on rock instead of shifting sands.

In the Bhagavad-Gita Arjuna asks Lord Krishna how one can distinguish the self-realized man from the natural man. And Krishna has this to say about the conduct of the enlightened:—

> Not shaken by adversity,
> Not hankering after happiness :
> Free from fear, free from anger,
> Free from the things of desire.
> I call him a seer, and illumined.
>
> The bonds of his flesh are broken,
> He is lucky, and does not rejoice :
> He is unlucky, and does not weep.
> I call him illumined.
>
> Water flows continually into the ocean
> But the ocean is never disturbed :

* *The First and Last Freedom*, London, Gollancz, 1956, p. 140.

Desire flows into the mind of the seer
But he is never disturbed.
The seer knows peace:
The man who stirs up his own lusts
Can never know peace.
He knows peace who has forgotten desire
He lives without craving:
Free from ego, free from pride.

This is the state of enlightenment in Brahman
A man does not fall back from it
Into delusion.
Even at the moment of death
He is alive in that enlightenment:
Brahman and he are one.

When we take the word 'lust' in its widest meaning, signifying 'lust for life', we recognize that the Lord Krishna has con-
trasted the same two opposing ways of life in this verse. He
who has entirely lost the lust for life has stopped the process
of becoming: he has no longer any ambitions, whether to
become rich, famous, or even holy or spiritual. He no longer
wants anything for himself for he has fully realized the
emptiness of what he wants as well as what constitutes his
'self'. Once again it is instructive to hear what Krishnamurti
has to say on this topic. He states: 'The wanting more, the
pursuit of symbols, words, images, with their sensations—
all that has to come to an end. Only then is it possible for the
mind to be in that state of creativeness in which the new
can always come into being. If you will understand without
being mesmerized by words, by habits, by ideas, and see how
important it is to have the new constantly impinging on the
mind, then perhaps you will understand the process of desire,
the routine, the boredom, the constant craving for experience. Then, I think, you will begin to see that desire has very
little significance in life for a man who is really seeking.
Obviously there are certain physical needs: food, clothing,
shelter, and all the rest of it. But they never become psychological appetites, things on which the mind builds itself as a
centre of desire.'*

In short, it can be said that the man who has liberated him-

* *Ibid*, p. 102.

self no longer has any desire to be, either psychologically or physiologically. When this desireless state has come about, the subject lives entirely in the present, in the eternal now —the most real and natural way of living, for the past and future exist only in our imagination: the past forms our memory and the future is merely a continuation of the past. Conversely every imaginative-emotive impression is always concerned with past or future. The words of Christ 'Take no heed for the morrow' and 'Let the dead bury their own' cease to be injunctions in the desireless state, for the subject has quite naturally arrived in the blessed condition that no heed for the morrow is taken and it is fully realized that the past is dead. Paradoxically enough it can be said that this state which is like living death†, the death of the Old Man, is at the same time the most intensive form of living possible! It is not as some people imagine, the extinction of life following upon the extinction of the ego—on the contrary, it is living with complete abandon, putting heart and soul into what one is actually doing at the moment. Just as the purpose of the dancer is the dance—and not going round the floor in order to get somewhere—so the purpose of what we are doing at any moment lies in the doing, and there are no second thoughts or ulterior motives to dilute the intensity of our actions.

Thus, it may be said that after enlightenment life is just as hectic as before; only with this difference that there is no personal involvement! (There is the deed, but no doer.) So we have the utmost, vigorous action side by side with complete peace of mind—surely, no better conditions for successful action can be envisaged. Being at the same time attuned to maximal inspiration, i.e. in a state of creativity, it need not be wondered, perhaps, that the enlightened person is effortlessly capable of the highest achievement. To a certain extent all great works of art have been the results of a certain 'grace' that has befallen their originators; in their moments of inspiration these artists have created without thought of

† Compare also the words of Christ: 'If anyone wants to follow in my footsteps *he must give up all right to himself* . . . For the man who wants to save his life will lose it, but the man who loses his life for my sake will save it.' (Luke 9: 23); one of the few places in the Gospels where Christ bluntly states that one of the necessary conditions for enlightenment is that the self be transcended and thus eliminated; he must let go of himself and stop clinging to life.

gain for the self, almost in spite of themselves: they just could not help themselves when creativity came over them.

This attitude of action without thought for its fruits one finds also in Krishnamurti's writings (where it is termed 'action without idea'; see also p. 19), and in the Gita:—

> United with Brahman,
> Cut free from the fruit of the act,
> A man finds peace
> in the work of the spirit,
> Without Brahman,
> Man is a prisoner,
> Enslaved by action,
> Dragged onward by desire.
>
> Happy is that dweller
> In the city of nine gates*
> Whose discrimination
> Has cut him free from his act:
> He is not involved in action
> He does not involve others.
>
> Do not say:
> 'God gave us this delusion'.
> You dream you are the doer,
> You dream that action is done,
> You dream that action bears fruit.
> It is your ignorance,
> It is the world's delusion
> That gives you these dreams.

And elsewhere we read:—

> The seers say truly
> That he is wise
> Who acts without lust or scheming
> For the fruit of the act:
> His act falls from him,
> Its chain is broken,
> Melted in the flame of my knowledge.
> Turning his face from the fruit,
> He needs nothing:

* The human body.

The Atman is enough.
He acts, and is beyond action.

What God's Will gives
He takes, and is contented.
Pain follows pleasure,
He is not troubled:
Gain follows loss,
He is indifferent:
Of whom should he be jealous?
He acts, and is not bound by his action.

When the bonds are broken
His illumined heart
Beats in Brahman:
His every action
Is worship of Brahman!
Can such acts bring evil?

This momentary and completely spontaneous and natural living without the pains of attachment or the tensions of anticipation is reminiscent of the state of purity which we once possessed as a child. We can now see why Christ upheld little children as our example, when he stated: 'Believe me, unless you change your whole outlook and become like little children you will never enter the Kingdom of Heaven' (Matthew 18:1).

Some people mistakenly think that, as said before, Nirvana means death, and consequently the extinction of all sensitivity towards beauty and the good things of life; they also think that this state is brought about by the repression of desire; but the Gita points out the fallacy of this way of thinking:—

The abstinent run away from what they desire
But carry their desires with them:
When a man enters Reality,
He leaves his desires behind him.

When a man leaves his desires behind him, or 'has forgotten them', as it says elsewhere in the Gita, surely, he must be free from them because he has destroyed delusion, ignorance: the origin and the emptiness of what he terms 'desires' has been revealed to him.* When in that state of understanding, of purity, he can enjoy the pleasures that come his way without reserve—for he is free and never attached, never enslaved by his experience. This situation has been very well summed up in the following beautiful verse, which occurs in Prof. Blyth's work, *Zen in English Literature and Oriental Classics:*—

> He who bends to himself a Joy,
> Doth the winged life destroy,
> But he who kisses the Joy as it flies,
> Lives in eternity's sunrise.

Contrary to the natural man, who lives superficially, in the periphery, the self-realized man lives from the centre of his being—and being at once the source and its manifestation, he is free. He lives in a state of creativity, inspiration, love; it is this love Christians denote by the word 'agapé'. Unlike ordinary so-called 'love' it is not an emotive state for it is a condition of complete detachment,** whereas emotion is always the opposite. It cannot really be described but perhaps one could say that it is more in the nature of a complete understanding, firstly of oneself, and as a result of this, an insight into the nature of the outside world, which is then seen to be the same as the 'self'. Buddhists call this love 'karuna', and according to Dr D. T. Suzuki, this is only another aspect of prajna, transcendental wisdom.

The man who has this love is capable of purely constructive action without thought of gain for himself—such action is also completely spontaneous and unpremeditated, and flows forth from the original source of his being, namely that which is at once personal and impersonal. Such a man will love his neighbour as himself—even if that neighbour professes to be his enemy; for loving him as oneself means transcending all duality, realizing that one's enemies—even when committing the greatest atrocities—are blinded by ignorance or, they act the way they do—to use the words of

* The first words of the Buddha after his enlightenment experience were: 'Desire, I know thy root, from imagination art thou born; no more shall I indulge in imagination, I shall have no desire any more.'
** On a deeper level it would be more accurate to talk of a condition which is neither attachment nor detachment, for both these terms are still in reference to a 'self'.

Christ—'for they do not know what they are doing'. In the
Gita we read : —

> He who regards
> With an eye that is equal
> Friends and comrades,
> The foe and the kinsman,
> The vile, the wicked,
> The men who judge him,
> And those who belong
> To neither faction :
> He is the greatest.

The self-realized man represents, psychologically, the final
stage of evolution of natural man, for he has attained the
highest degree of adaptation, perfect harmony with his sur-
rounding. Paradoxically enough, by having lost his fear of
death, he has increased his survival value. Through having
fully understood the faculty of self-consciousness, by which
man distinguishes himself from the animals, he has turned
something that is ever present in natural man as a potential
if not active source of neurosis, into a positive blessing: a
means of knowing and realizing his own divine nature.

5

THOUGHT AND REALIZATION

Books on Zen Buddhism usually discuss the subject on a fairly advanced plane. The dialogues of Zen masters with monks generally concern the state of the man who has had or is about to have satori. For beginners to seek truth by studying this kind of book is therefore like putting the cart before the horse. All works on Zen stress that it is necessary for man to stop conceptualized thought, i.e. to 'slay' the mind or to bring thought to an end completely. In that, they conform, of course, with what Krishnamurti has said. Now it seems to me that to 'learn' to do this, books are of no use whatever. One does not quieten an agitated mind by absorbing information from books; this only adds to the agitation and confusion. The stilling of the mind comes about only through self-knowledge, leading to the self coming to nought.

Before we can understand the stilling of the mind through self-knowledge we should try to understand the process of thought, in particular its birth. Krishnamurti states that thought comes about when experience is insufficiently or incompletely understood, giving rise to 'psychological residue' (which in plain English means: the clinging to some habitual thought pattern). This psychological residue or memory gets revitalized when challenged by the present—giving rise to the illusion of the 'self' (which is the sum total of habitual thought patterns with which intelligence has identified itself) and the sufferings ensuing from that concept.

Zen writings as exemplified by *The Zen Teaching of Huang-Po on the Transmission of Mind* state that thought comes about when the mind dwells on and is held by the phenomena (cf., Krishna to Arjuna: 'All human beings are led astray from the moment they are born for thinking this relative world is real'). This does not mean that the mind should turn away from the phenomenal world as being a hindrance; it should simply regard all phenomena as equally important or equally unimportant. Huang-Po says we should regard all things with an equal eye 'as though we are too ill to bother' about any in particular. Thus the mind does not dwell on any particular phenomenal aspect of the world; hence there is no concept formation; no identification with phenomena. Usually certain phenomena are considered more important than others and we are held by them. Which are those phenomena? If we look into this we find they are always phenomena that bear some direct relation to the up-keep of the 'self' (this may be by giving the subject the impression of self-affirmation, or by 'threatening' the conscious and unconscious mechanisms of self-affirmation).

The natural question to ask at this point is 'How has the concept of the self come about in the first place?' It has come about through identification. For example, I always observe phenomena in their interaction with 'my' body or 'my' consciousness. The heat makes 'me' sweat; in this case there is identification with my body: 'me' is 'my body'. We see how the *heat* affects and apparently causes *the sweating of the body*. Hence we assume these are two separate things interacting; the Zen person on the other hand does not differentiate. To him both 'phenomena' are one process, for the sweating is 'caused' as much by the nature of the sweat glands as by the heat. (Superficially, there seems to be cause and effect, but on a deeper level it is difficult to see where cause ends and effect begins.)

Or in any psychological experience, such as experiencing likes and dislikes, there is identification with my physico-psychological organism. For example, somebody has insulted me, in which case there is identification with the image (memory) I carry in my consciousness of 'myself' and which I cherish: the image is belittled, perhaps mutilated so as to be almost unrecognizable, so 'I' feel the pain. In both cases I have created the 'me' and the 'mine'. It is the same with the basic process of desire that takes place along the following lines: perception—→ contact —→ identification —→ desire —→ frustration or gratification. So we see that Krishnamurti's 'revitalization of psychological residue', Huang-Po's 'dwelling on phenomena', and the processes of desire and aversion are in reality one and the same thing: the up-keep of the false concept of the 'self' through the mechanism of identification.

When we dwell upon phenomena it is with a view to changing them. Memory actually does not accept what *is*, but wants to interfere using knowledge which is based on the past (this is how likes and dislikes come about). This tension between what is and what is not is the suffering. But if we completely understand this mechanism and stay with our suffering, undergo it as a complete experience, we shall realize that there is only this tension, 'suffering', and no sufferer. If, on the other hand, we ignore or repress suffering, or try to escape from it, we create the 'sufferer' and thus pro-long and intensify the suffering.

It must be clear now that we can never be free until we give up clinging to phenomena. For once we are free from phenomena there is no conceptualized thought; there is no consciousness of being a self: the mind is in a fluid state free from emotional blockages, which means that there is full awareness of phenomena only, without condemnation or justification which introduces an evaluation on an 'absolute' scale. Basically, it is therefore the phenomena that bind us— i.e. the illusion of their absolute reality. The mind should observe the phenomenal world in much the same way that the beam of a television camera scans the image projected on to it from the outside world (cf. Takuan's injunction not to 'stop' the mind*). Only thus can we perceive a true and un-distorted picture of the world. Only then do we truly live in the Void—what is more, we have become the Void.

* Takuan on Zen and swordsmanship :—
'Not to move means not to 'stop' with an object that is seen. For as it is seen it passes on and the mind is not arrested. When the mind 'stops' with each object as it is presented, the mind is disturbed with all kinds of thought and feeling. The 'stopping' inevitably leads to the moving that is disturbance. Though the mind is thus subject to 'stoppings', it in itself remains unmoved . . ." (D. T. Suzuki, *Zen and Japanese Culture*, London, Routledge, 1959, p. 98.)
In this connection it may also be observed that the injunction not to fabricate concepts, stressed so much by Zen, is reminiscent of the Buddha's description of the enlightened state, when in the seen there is only the seeing, in the heard only the hearing.

6

IDEATION AND PERCEPTION

Understanding is a function that resembles seeing more than anything else; its mechanism is really nothing more than an extension of 'seeing with the eyes' (for even this 'seeing' actually takes place in the brain). (It is interesting to note the wisdom occasionally contained in language: we say colloquially 'I see' for 'I understand.')

Ideas act like screens which obscure that which has to be seen; therefore, ideation hinders understanding, perception of Reality. This is the reason why in Zen, and in the statements of nearly all religious thinkers, so much emphasis is placed on the emptying of the mind.

When we speak of liberation we actually mean freedom from fear, from anxiety, which as Kierkegaard has observed, lies continually at the root of all modern man's experience. This fear is in fact nothing else but our subjection to one or more concepts of the mind; e.g. 'if such and such is going to happen it threatens me', implies various unspoken assumptions or concepts: firstly the concept of 'me' and secondly the concept of the vulnerability of that postulated 'me'. If we reflect one moment we shall see that these concepts are the results of conditioning by society, by our upbringing, etc.; they have not always been there as is witnessed by the peculiar carefree, happy-go-lucky existence of childhood. One moment we were happy and smiled, the next we cried in our sadness—but our joy and sadness were momentary: they were not carried over into time because they did not become fixations in the brain. Our existence was then unfettered by concepts, by ideation, and fear of certain dangerous situations had to be carefully inculcated by our parents and teachers. Of course, now, from the superior adult position we disdainfully call the behaviour of the young infant animal-like—as though we could divide Nature so easily in animal-like and God-like manifestations. Is not this schism artificial, a concept of the mind, also?

Hence, in order to free ourselves from fear it is simply a logical necessity that we first free ourselves from philosophizing, from carrying concepts with us in our minds for only through this activity has the mind become our own prison. Once the mind lets go its ceaseless activities, i.e. its playing about with concepts, and stops the process of ideation, we are at once free and in the Void—or rather the Void comes into being for we no longer carry the burden of our selves!

Now in order to be free from concepts and ideas we must go into the process of ideation and see this process actually taking place in our mind; so that we fully realize that ideation is a fabrication of the mind, and not a facet of absolute reality. Since this seeing of the process of ideation is just as easily hindered by ideation itself as any other perception of impersonal reality, this capability presupposes a certain quietness of mind, a certain openness to the truth. It is on account of this vicious circle, that observing the process of our own thought is so extremely difficult, although inherently it is a simple seeing like any other form of perception.

When we observe impartially the process of ideation taking place in ourselves we find that this is a secondary process, a process that comes at a stage subsequent to perception; this was hidden from us by the lightning speed with which mental processes take place. Ideation is the process of naming, classifying, and correlating that which has been perceived—it is the process of a mind that can only 'see' things in a particular way, according to the pattern of its conditioning. Therefore, if we try to perceive reality and intermingle this activity with that of ideation, we are confounding two different levels of reality. The result of this confusion is that instead of 'understanding' we come to some 'interpretation' (which is something totally different) of an incompletely understood objective reality.

To give an example of our concept-consciousness. At the time the author is writing this it is spring, and the whole of nature seems to be caught in a spurt of creativity; the birds sing their liveliest song and out in the country there is a perfume in the air. Now is there creativity all at once because it has turned spring? Of course not. The Zen person would point out that this is just as much nonsense as saying that the cold makes me shiver. The cold and 'shivering' are one process, and just so are spring and the renewal of nature one. The one does not cause the other—they are coexistent but the one could not exist but for the other. The point is that human experience is determined as much by the nature of the mind and the structure of the sense organs as by the external phenomena that are being perceived. This is again another form of expressing Nagarjuna's doctrine of Sunyavada; our thinking in time, in terms of cause and effect, is the result of ideation, and from the eternal point of view the concept of causality is void, too.

The most poisonous concept of all is probably the teleological one, that of purpose, which all the time presupposes something over and beyond life, as though life by itself with its infinite variety of phenomena were of insufficient interest. It is insidious because it binds the person who holds it to the concepts of past and future, and blinds him to the only Reality, that which exists here and now. Such a person would suggest, for instance, that the birds sing *because* they want to communicate with each other in their bird language. Well, maybe they do communicate, but that is not the point.

Basically, however, all ideation is harmful because concepts hypnotize us into faulty perception and wrongful thinking. It divides the individual against himself and separates him from the rest of creation. The first schism it creates is that of the self versus the non-self, which gives rise to man's feeling of isolation, his inability to feel part of Nature expressed so very revealingly in his wish to 'conquer' Nature. And of course, it does not stop at that because the process of ideation, once started, is very difficult to end, for it *is* the mind. So, the self further divides itself into good and bad, godly and devilish, conscious and unconscious, etc.— thus causing man to be at war with his own humanity. This insidious situation has been well summed up in Hsin-hsin Ming, the oldest Zen poem, by Seng-ts'an:—

> A split hair's difference,
> And heaven and earth are set apart!

> If you want to get the plain truth,
> Be not concerned with right and wrong.
> The conflict between right and wrong
> Is the sickness of the mind.*

This same 'plain truth' is, of course, also expressed in Christ's injunction 'Judge not' (which includes the judging of 'oneself'), but few of the so-called practising Christians today seem to be mindful of it, nor do they seem to be aware that the real meaning of Christ's coming lay in his victory over righteousness. They miss the whole point of Christianity which is contained in the shift in emphasis from the 'Law' to the insights afforded by the 'Holy Spirit' (i.e. the spiritual life), from the world of thought, ideation, to the life of the spirit, where stark illogicalities like 'Love thy enemy' (as well as other pairs of opposites) can be transcended, and start making sense. For this was the real innovation of Christianity over Judaism, and so upsetting was its impact on the established Church, that its instigator could only end like so many other great revolutionaries had ended, by laying down his life.

So we see, that when 'heaven and earth are set apart', there is ever the struggle between what *is* and what *should be*, the brooding on the 'self', respectably called 'introspection', and all the other egotistic activities which aim at improving, perfecting oneself. The perfection of Zen on the other hand is to be perfectly and simply human:—

> We eat, excrete, sleep and get up;
> This is our world.
> All we have to do after that—
> Is to die.—
>
>   Ikkyu[1]

It is the perfection which is implied when Zen Buddhists state that we have been Buddhas from the moment we were born, or that we have been 'created in God's image' as Christians would put it. It is not only the perfection of Zen and Christianity, however, but also that of Taoism, for according to Chuang-tzu:—

* A. W. Watts, *The Way of Zen*, p. 115.

'The baby looks at things all day without winking; that is because his eyes are not focused on any particular object. He goes without knowing where he is going, and stops without knowing what he is doing. *He merges himself with the surroundings and moves along with it.* These are the principles of mental hygiene.'[2] (Italics are mine, R.P.)

And also the following beautiful passage seems revelant:—

'If you regulate your body and unify your attention, the harmony of heaven will come upon you. If you integrate your awareness, and unify your thoughts, spirit will make its abode with you. *Te* (virtue) will clothe you, and the Tao will shelter you. Your eyes will be like those of a new-born calf, which seeks not the wherefore.'[3] (It is interesting to see the parallel of the last sentence with the symbolism of the lamb in the story of Jesus).

For the person who has Zen there is neither the self nor the non-self, neither the One nor the Many. The process that moves his little finger is the same as that which causes earthquakes and thunderstorms; the process by which he breathes, or—as he experiences it—which 'breathes' him, is the same as that by which thoughts come and go. Hearing the birds sing outside his window, he is just as much producing that bird song as he is being himself. It is not that he thinks this way (for then again it would be the result of ideation) but he feels it with his whole being, although 'feeling', for lack of a better word, is to be understood in this connection as 'experiencing' that which is not thought and not emotion. The same fundamental Zen experience of non-duality is, of course, also reflected in that tremendous saying by Christ: 'In so far as you are doing this unto the least of my brethren you are doing it to me.'

All individual and collective suffering can be seen to be the result of ideation. Where there is ideation, there is definition, where there is definition there are divisions and labels—the labels then become slogans and banners; the banners so easily become 'causes'—and then causes for war and all the other miseries such as concentration camps, brain-washings, atom bombs, etc. But not only does this process of division operate on the political level, it does so on any level, for ideation excludes love. On the so-called religious level, for example, we are either Christians or Buddhists, either this or that. To at least most of us, it has never occurred that we could be both Christians and Buddhists, that there are neither Christian nor Buddhist truths, but that, in fact, all truth just *is*, although this truth may be translated into either Christian or Buddhist terminology.

When this insight has been attained, we see the futility, the childishness as well as the dangers of labelling ourselves, and we then cease to erect barriers around ourselves. Here again it is instructive to realize how little labels meant for Christ, when we see how he mixed with Samaritans, and various other people like tax-collectors, prostitutes, etc., who were considered definitely Non-U in his days. Let us finally see what Krishnamurti has to say on this topic:—'It is the immediate perception of truth that is liberating, not ideation. Ideas merely breed further ideas, and ideas are not in any way going to give happiness to man. Only when ideation ceases is there being; and being is the solution.'*

* *Krishnamurti's Talks*, Bombay, 1948.
[1] Transl. R. H. Blyth in 'Ikkyu's Doka', *The Young East*, 2, No. 7 (Tokyo, 1953).
[2] A. W. Watts, op. cit., p. 23.
[3] *Ibid.*, p. 102.

7

EMPTINESS

The term emptiness as used in everyday life has two distinctly different connotations. When used in the literal sense it always refers to material things. But it may also be used figuratively, when it has the sense of meaninglessness, futility, expressing a feeling of boredom and perhaps even despair.

In Zen, which seems to thrive on paradox, turning things upside down and inside out, the word emptiness is used in a unique manner: there, it refers to a mental state but in the sense which, in everyday life, it carries only when speaking of material things. When we speak of emptiness of the mind as a prerequisite for satori, we may very easily be misunderstood by the ordinary person who is not familiar with the terminology—a terminology, which, it must be added, is hardly adequate to express such an unusual and unimaginable 'concept' as that of a mind free from all concepts, even that of emptiness! Perhaps the best definition of this 'state of mind' was given by Te-shan, in the following lines:—

> 'Only when you have no thing in your mind
> and no mind in things, are you vacant
> and spiritual, empty and marvellous.'*

How does this unique state, this emptiness, come about? It comes about only when the mind has exhausted itself, come to the end of its tethers, in realizing to the fullest its own emptiness (here used in the conventional sense of the word). The whole Zen experience of enlightenment can, therefore, be summed up as the 'going from "emptiness"

* H. Dumoulin and R. F. Sasaki, *The Development of Chinese Zen after the Sixth Patriarch*, New York, First Zen Institute, 1953, p. 48.

through emptiness to Reality', or as Krishnamurti expressed it, equally paradoxically: 'Let your heart be wholly empty; then only will it be filled.' We can also clearly see the underlying analogy of the cup which can only be used properly when empty: the mind is an efficient instrument only when in this condition.

8

ON MINDFULNESS

The process of mindfulness could perhaps most aptly be designated by the term 'objectification', i.e. the depersonalizing of the experience of the 'I', the subjective experience, and making it objective. This entails drawing an ever wider circle around the 'I' and observing it in its relationships. Ignorance is objectivity within too narrow an area. For instance I may think that the sun moves around the earth—for within the narrow circle of my experience this is an objective fact. Once I broaden my sphere of observation and I look upon the earth/sun configuration from a point of view, say, outside the solar system, I see that it is actually the other way round: that it is the earth which moves around the sun.

This example is instructive because it shows there are different levels of reality in our thinking and although within their framework of reference both observations were objective, the wider field of observation produces a finding which is more 'true' than the narrower one. This process is essentially that of the evolution of scientific thought with the replacement of one working hypothesis after another, without ever passing out of the sphere of relative truth into that of absolute and unconditional Truth. It demonstrates clearly the relativity of all concepts, the fundamental emptiness of all propositions because they are always based on relativities, and as much the reflection of the properties of the mind and the sense organs (in other words, the limitations of the observer) as of the 'realities' of Nature.

What applies to the observation of so-called physical phenomena applies also to the observation of psychological phenomena, in finding out about ourselves—but here, ignorance produces suffering. For example, in considering my affairs, my relations with the outside world, all my experiences confirm me in thinking that everything revolves around me: *I* rejoice, *I* suffer, etc. I appear to be the centre of the Universe. Even if bitter experience contradicts this egocentric world view and I experience 'suffering', I cannot face up to it and immediately switch on the imagination in which the 'I' fabricates for itself the dominating position for which it craves and without which it could not envisage life. (Hubert Benoit calls this process the 'mechanism of compensations' in his book on Zen Buddhism.)

But now what happens if I stop this process and reverse it? As soon as I look in on myself 'from the outside', that is from the point of view of an objective onlooker, an entirely different picture presents itself—a picture in which I figure hardly at all. I may for example be in conflict with another person. Looking at it subjectively the main field of my consciousness is filled with the picture of my enemy, with all its emotional associations of hatred, fear, etc. But if I can look at the situation from outside myself, attention becomes focused on the conflict itself. Then what happens? The more I go into it, the more I understand conflict by facing the *total* situation, the less I feel the pain of it, the less I am emotionally or intellectually involved. Instead of merely naming the conflict, naming the hatred for my opponent, etc., and thereby strengthening these feelings (by the emotional associations of the words) without coming to terms with them, I now stay with the pain of conflict, the pain of fear, and by living it to the full, becoming that pain, come to an understanding which is not merely verbal—and so become free from it.

So what happens in awareness is that thought becomes continually less self-centred, less crude and more subtle. I become more and more an objective onlooker with respect to my affairs, for I have no longer a vested interest in the results of 'my' thought processes; therefore there is no longer a fixed point from which all thinking proceeds: only thought following upon thought, and the 'I' is no longer important. Eventually I realize what I am: a psychological disturbance; thought comes to an end and things are 'seen' directly and in full clarity—this happens when the thinker and the thought become one.

The process of mindfulness or awareness can be summed

up in the following way. As I observe myself in the mirror of relationship, the 'absolute' character of my motives, aspirations, desires, etc., is undermined for they are now seen as conditioned responses—this takes the ground away from under them. Consciousness now only recognizes a network of thoughts and emotions in interplay, and this observation produces a peculiar change in outlook. 'All is emptiness', the feeling of involvement and commitment of my desires revolves from me; I feel there is no solid foundation for any of the habitual reactions that strengthen the 'me' and the 'mine'. There still are the emotions, but instead of saying 'I am happy', 'I suffer', I would say 'There is happiness', 'There is suffering', and I no longer want to or feel I ought to do anything about it. In other words: there is no self and I am now intensely aware of the falseness of the notion of the self. There is only thought, and thought about a self, but that self has no absolute reality apart from being a concept in the mind.

Once I realize this truth in the observation of my responses—and this is something entirely different from a mere intellectual acceptance of the doctrine of 'anatta' (or no-self)—then I am free for I am no longer worried about what is going to happen to something that I no longer experience as 'something', an 'I' with which I am no longer concerned because I am no longer identified with it—and as soon as I am no longer concerned I am no longer strengthening the 'me' at its centre. Hence my actions and thoughts are no longer imprisoned within the limits of the ego; there is the beginning of freedom.

Through mindfulness each emotion is neutralized as it crops up, thus preventing the emotive state with its attachments. Phenomena now appear as pure phenomena only, and no longer create bondage by their impositions of value judgments. One is so little tied up with them, there is such an inner tranquillity that it appears almost as if one is 'too ill to bother' (to use the words of Huang-Po) with phenomena that formerly used to throw one into fits of excitement—this is true serenity. Everything happens as though it does not concern 'me'; since I am so much part and parcel of these happenings there is no relationship with them. Or to put it slightly differently: I am not affected because the 'me' does not exist separately from the events.

This mindfulness or awareness is not something that has to or can be practised; it comes to the awakened man spontaneously in the same way that, say, beautiful music evokes a response in the sensitive listener. Awareness is thought becoming aware of thought, i.e. the way in which thought occurs in patterns which are brought about and cultivated by desire, the desire to keep intact this illusory entity, the thinker. Awareness acting on this process brings it to an end.

THE PARADOX IN MINDFULNESS

We would like to forget ourselves but in order to do this we ought to pursue every thought to its end, so that it leaves no psychological residue. However, to complete a thought does not mean 'thinking', for this would only mean the birth of further thoughts—but staying with the thought without naming it and thus going beyond the verbal level. Only in this manner will its hidden meaning be intimated to us, and only then shall we be able to completely 'forget' that thought or 'emotion'—once we have seen clearly what *is*. We then also perceive that every thought cropping up within the framework of pain and pleasure flows forth directly from the idea we carry of ourselves, the ego. Had we no idea of ourselves, no such thoughts would arise, the mind would be empty—the emptiness talked of by Shi-tou: 'vacant and spiritual, empty and marvellous'.

However, there is a vicious circle at work here, for the thoughts and emotions form the ego just as much as vice versa. This vicious circle—and with it the ego—can only be broken, when we complete each thought, or in other words, by perfect self-knowledge, which is the total understanding of our mental processes and their origination.

THE SELF AND ITS LIBERATION

(Representing mainly a summary of Krishnamurti's teaching)

When Krishnamurti talks about thought arising through revivification of a psychological residue—the latter being the result of incomplete understanding of experience—he is referring to that whole complex of thoughts, feelings and emotions which represent our acquisitions, hopes, fears, desires, etc., that together make up the self (and without which the 'me' would simply not be at all). Unless we thoroughly understand the origin and significance of each of these thoughts and feelings they will persist. This bundle of thoughts and emotions gives itself continuity by means of time, that is, the process of recognition and accumulation, the desire always to become something different from what is now. (For instance, at present I recognize I am 'evil' and I must be 'good', and I think that for this transformation I need time, which means that through certain efforts I can gradually accumulate goodness and thus change from bad to good).

The effort towards continuity, towards psychological security is always accompanied by fear—the fear to be negated, not to succeed in one's efforts of transformation, in becoming something either positively or negatively. This fear cannot be overcome, for what is conquered once must be conquered again and again. Fear *is* the mind—the process of consciousness to divide itself and to give continuity to this division. That is why Krishnamurti can state: 'The function of the mind is to be separated. Otherwise your mind is simply not there.'* The feeling of separateness, the desire

* *The First and Last Freedom*, p. 117.

to be—either psychologically or religio-politically—*is* the fear. Therefore, if the mind tries to conquer fear it is endeavouring the impossible—for by its own action it can only strengthen itself. Fear can only go spontaneously, and this happens only when the mind has become utterly still. The mind cannot be forced to become still, but it is spontaneously quiet when the whole process of consciousness has been completely understood.

It may then be asked what new factor comes into being, when the mind is utterly still. The answer to this question is that nothing new comes into being, but a state of Consciousness or Intelligence prevails *which is neither individual nor collective*. This state prevails because it is no longer covered with Ignorance, which is Consciousness being oriented into an individual frame of reference, so that the empirical ego continually 'uses' that Intelligence for its own ends, having in the first place created this 'individual frame of reference' (the ego), which then becomes its own prison. This cyclic process* is the unhappy by-product of the emergence of self-consciousness, which came about in the course of evolution to give individual Man a better chance of physical survival. But factual memory led to psychological memory—and so the physical needs to psychological desires, and the urge for physical self-preservation to the desire to protect the integrity of the 'personality'—thus giving rise to man as an animal that suffers frustration through its own specialization.

The field of consciousness is no longer a homogeneous continuum, it is heterogeneous: warped and twisted by 'I-consciousness'. We can now see that to talk of 'union' with God or Reality achieved by the 'liberated' man is a metaphorical way of speaking, which is actually quite misleading and not helpful to our understanding. For nothing is achieved and there is no union, since there is no entity that can achieve union with anything else; nor is there any 'liberation'. There is the loosening of the 'knot' in the continuum of consciousness and the return of the individual mind to Nothingness; there is the stepping out of time, for the time-binding process of becoming has come to an end; there is purely the being of the timeless continuum. But let us forget all metaphors and

*This is further examined on p. 54.

images, for they produce new attachments and illusions, standing in the way of Nothingness.

The cyclic process, discussed on p. 53, will now be looked into in a slightly different and somewhat more detailed manner:—

Self-consciousness presupposes desire/fear, for the 'I' cannot live except in separation, in opposition, in duality. At the same time fear and desire depend upon self-consciousness, are inherent with it. The more the ego succeeds in crystallizing out, in strengthening itself, the more it becomes aware of the threat of the non-self to its permanence—hence fear increases. René Fouéré mentions the following links in a cyclic process: *self-consciousness⟶ basic fear⟶ desire for security⟶ greed⟶ acquisitions*. Each of these terms can be seen in a cyclic relationship with any of the others. For example, it may be said with equal accuracy that greed is the cause of fear and also that fear is the cause of greed. About this relationship Fouéré states further: 'What exists is a self-activating movement, which contains all its causes within itself. This point should not be lost from view if one wants truly to understand Krishnamurti's approach. Otherwise it may appear full of contradictions . . . The fact that self-consciousness in the shape of the "I" and "mine" is the product from moment to moment of a cyclic process which feeds on itself is one of the great discoveries of Krishnamurti. Both the strangeness and the gravity of the implications are breath-taking.'*

* *Krishnamurti—The Man and his Teaching*, Bombay, Chetana, 1958, p. 48-51.

II

THE VICIOUS CIRCLE

In the study of mental processes we come up time and again against a situation which is called a 'vicious circle'—and indeed a very vicious state this is when psychological. The following seems to me such a situation. In order to understand anything at all, we need intelligence. I am not now discussing the intellectual sharpness required to see a process of logical deduction to its end, the process of ideation—but I am referring to this creative intelligence which is capable of understanding the new and unfamiliar, that which cannot be deduced from the old, namely the 'here and now'. This intelligence only comes about when the self is in abeyance. When the self is strong there is not this intelligence. And for the self to be in abeyance also a certain intelligence is needed, namely to see the self as it really is, in its ceaseless activities. For it is only when we have become aware of the self that there is the possibility of being free from it. Therefore, for the person with a strong ego—and he is the only one who can transcend it—it is humanly impossible to obtain this faculty of 'prajna'—this deep insight which is not knowledge.

Yet, we can now understand that when the vicious circle does break, the process of enlightenment is sudden and not progressive, for intelligence and the dissolving of the self strengthen each other as in a chain reaction. Perhaps the only factor that can break the vicious circle, that acts like a catalyst, is interest, the 'spirit of enquiry', as it is termed in Zen. Because when we are really interested in something for its own sake, the self automatically lies low; it is temporarily displaced by the object with which there is complete communion. Then only are we capable of looking quietly at the thing that interests us, without interposing our ideas about it.

It is in that passive yet alert state that intelligence becomes available to us—and this is not the cleverness or intellectual acuity with which we are or are not endowed from birth. It is a state of Intelligence which transcends all personal assets —hence the spiritual life is not more difficult for the 'simple' person than it is for the intellectual or 'clever' person. Owing to the nature of the above depicted vicious circle the normal unenlightened state tends to perpetuate itself; however, the urge to seek truth for its own sake tends to increase clarity: 'Seek and ye shall find'.

REALITY AND ILLUSION

'Like visions in a dream, so must we regard all things'—
NAGARJUNA
(The closing words of the *Prajnaparamita*)

When enquiring into the relationship between mind and Mind—the self and Buddhahood—one may use the following analogy. Supposing we throw a stone into some stationary water; immediately waves emerge and apparently start to travel outwards from the centre of the disturbance. They are of increasing radius and they in turn produce secondary waves when meeting an obstacle. This is exactly how thought, the self, operates. Both mechanisms are illusory. The waves travelling outwards are of course an optical illusion, caused by the synchronous up-and-down movements of the water particles in a certain pattern. Otherwise these particles, with regard to their distance from the centre of disturbance, are quite stationary. Just so is the self only a ripple, a momentary disturbance in Mind, which is called the Unborn. Illusion and deception set in as soon as we consider that the waves have an existence separate from the water, or the 'experiences' as being different from the 'experiencer', instead of realizing that *the waves are the water, the experiences and the experiencer are one*. As the water manufactures the optical illusion of the waves, so thought creates the illusion of the thinker.

Time also is an illusion: for without memory would we know time? Memory is basically the capacity of the protoplast to retain, to store an excitation—a feature of organic life of the greatest significance to its survival and second in importance only to the fact of the excitability itself, which one may call the hall-mark of the living protoplast. Now when we remember, we play back the excitation; therefore, in this aspect we are nothing more than a tape recording. Some people may say: but when we remember, we have a pretty good idea of the time interval since it was recorded. Is this not 'time'? Are we not more in this respect than a tape recording? Do we not carry with us a real 'sense of time' as a primeval reality, as 'psychological time'?

If your tape recording has been made a long time ago, it loses its clarity, its loudness. Just so with memory. Do we not say: 'I remember as clearly as yesterday'—indicating that apart from the intensity of the original impact of the engram there is a significant correlation between the clarity of the play-back of memory and the time interval during which it has been stored. Of course, this is not the full story. Being surrounded by clocks and calendars as we are, we continually keep a check on 'chronological time', and these checks too, we remember as dates, times, etc., together with a scale of chronological time—in much the same way that we plot the course of a scientific experiment against a time-base in a graph. So we continually strengthen the illusion of time as something that exists independently of us.

In reality it is the mind's own invention, for nothing but experience exists, which we call 'now', in relation to what is not: past and future. It will be appreciated that the 'now', as the idea of some 'point' in time, has come about as another concept, on the same level with past and future—by postulating a dividing line between past and future, and calling the point of intersection the 'present moment'. So ultimately there is neither past, present, nor future as time, there is only the experience of that which *is*, the 'eternal now', if you like. The 'movement' of time, as we normally understand it, is only made possible by memory, which, having created the past, projects out of itself, first the future, and then the present, as dimensions on a time-scale. In summing up we may say:—

Time = Memory = A property of the protoplast to retain physico-chemical changes in its substance.

This is an important conclusion, for normally we rely heavily on time. For instance we assume that 'in time' we may understand, we may become a 'better' person (time being the transforming factor), etc.; or we say in the course of a process of evolution a better society will eventually be created. The 'better' society will come but it will be a society based on the replacement of one set of conditionings by another. It may therefore be a better society from the conventional point of view, but it will still be based on the illusion of 'I' consciousness and therefore contain the seed of its eventual disintegration. The really different society, that is, a community of people living in Truth, in Reality and not in Delusion, can only come about by a revolution—the inward revolution whereby the individual steps resolutely out of time, i.e. lets go of the process of becoming.

Life is like a cinematographic film; the mind can only apprehend it in small dosages: by examining frame by frame, i.e. moment by moment; and like the movie film projector creates the illusion of movement, so the mind creates the illusion of past, present and future, simply because it is incapable of perceiving reality in any other way than in a space-time framework. But this is not surprising when we remember that the mind itself, self-consciousness, is the result of continuity, of time, and therefore can never go beyond its own limitations and perceive that which is timeless; in final analysis there is only thought which is transient.

Now we have looked into the nature of time the next logical step is to examine that of 'space'; for if time is something which the mind has invented, is there space? Space is the result of the concept of time, or vice versa. We say an object travels from point *A* to point *B* in space, needing a duration of time*; but if the latter does not exist the phenomenon of movement is an illusion**—and therefore

---

* The following Zen anecdote appears appropriate:—

One day as Hyakujo stepped out of the house with his Master, Baso, they saw a flight of wild geese. Baso asked: 'Where are they flying?' 'They have already flown away, Master.' Suddenly Baso seized Hyakujo by the nose and twisted it. Overcome by pain, Hyakujo cried out: 'O, oh!'

'You say they have flown away,' said Baso, 'but they have all been here from the beginning.'

Then Hyakujo's back ran with sweat, and he had *satori*. (Suzuki, *Zen Buddhism and Its Influence on Japanese Culture*, Kyoto, Eastern Buddhist Society, 1938.)

** That the conclusion we have arrived at so laboriously here can be a direct and immediate insight in Zen is shown by the following quotation from *The Sutra of Wei Lang*, London, Luzac, 1944, p. 24:—

'At that time Bhikkhu Yen Chung, Master of the Dharma, was lecturing on the Maha Parinirvana Sutra in the Temple. It happened that one day, when a pennant was blown about by the wind, two Bhikkhus entered

the background required for this phenomenon to take place in, 'space', is illusory, too. (See also footnote on p. 129.)

Looking at it very simply, it should not be difficult to understand that both space and time are the results of the nature of our retina, eye nerve and brain function—that there is only sense impression, experience, which is always in the 'Now'. Hence Krishnamurti states:—

'The "Now" is all existence. It contains the whole of time and space. In it are immortality, eternity, the future, the past, present, everything. All are contained in that for the man who is not afraid to conquer that separateness which he must eventually overcome . . .'

Similarly, it can be shown that also desire is an illusion, a big hoax; and all psychological desire will appear to be in the nature of a conditioned reflex (cf. Pavlov's experiments with dogs on the conditioned reflex). In the same way it can be shown that *all* dualistic thinking leads to illusion, the conventional ways of describing Reality are 'Maya' (unreal), and the logical outcome of such an enquiry is ultimately the Void. This approach leads thus to the same end as Nagarjuna's Sunyavada, as all true approaches must.

into a dispute as to what it was that was in motion, the wind or the pennant. As they could not settle their difference I submitted to them that it was neither, and that what actually moved was their own mind.'

13

LIVING IN THE VOID

Entering the Void is not only a most difficult transition stage, it is also initially a very painful experience. Realizing the Void in our mind, we can see clearly that at the same time the negative factors, the more obvious sources of suffering, are cut out of our lives, so also are the positive factors: from the crudest to the most subtle pleasures, the many things we used to 'look forward to'. This feeling of emptiness, blankness, is tantamount to experiencing a great ache, a feeling of despair. It is only when we have left the world of thought completely and find ourselves right in the Void, when we have become the Void, that this ache ceases, because it is caused by a remnant of the urge for fulfilment. However rarefied or subtle this desire may be at this stage, it is still there and will remain there, until the experiencer, the ego, has completely gone. Until that has happened there is the fear of being completely absorbed by the Void, the fear of nothingness, or rather the fear of losing the old, familiar life, the breaking of so many habits.

It appears humanly impossible to stop living for and begin living. This is the phase indicated in Zen terminology by 'The Great Doubt' which precedes satori. Yet occasionally—mostly in our childhood—we have experienced quite spontaneously and unexpectedly moments when the mere fact of being alive was pure bliss and we wanted nothing further. Perhaps then, the really great discovery man can make in his life is that the highest form of happiness is open even to him who has or is nothing—or just because he is nothing. The Japanese language is, I think, the only one which has a term for the experience of this state of being, the word 'wabi', probably the most exquisite word in any language. Maybe also, we find it expressed in the little verse about the ninth

century Zen master Pang Chü-shih, who, having nothing,
lived continuously in the Void:—

> Old Pang requires nothing in the world :
> All is empty with him, even a seat he has not,
> For absolute Emptiness reigns in his household;
> How empty indeed it is with no treasures!
> When the sun is risen, he walks through Emptiness,
> When the sun sets, he sleeps in Emptiness;
> Sitting in Emptiness he sings his empty songs,
> And his empty words reverberate through Emptiness.*

* D. T. Suzuki, *Essays in Zen Buddhism*, Vol. 2, p. 297; London, Luzac,
1927, 1933, 1934, reprinted Rider, 1949, 1950, 1951.

14

THE WAY WHICH IS NO-WAY

Sooner or later, most of us, I think, will come to discover that to a large extent life is suffering—that is, life as we know it. It is only when we die to this world, when the old Adam is no longer, that there is the end of suffering. But this not only means the end of all attachments to worldly things, but most difficult of all: the end of all attachment to the 'I', to the centre of the 'me'. For as long as there is still a shred of the 'I' in evidence, we are vulnerable, completely at the mercy of external circumstances—however much we try to control these, or think we have control over them.

The important point to be realized is that *dukkha*, suffering or frustration, is caused not by the individual trying to obtain too much control over his environment, but by *any* effort on his part to exercise control in order to defend his peace of mind or seek happiness. Any such action is conducive to suffering for it is a process that only leads to a strengthening of the self. Unfortunately for us, in the spiritual life there is no halfway house—this life brooks no compromise and can only be approached when we begin to be completely honest with ourselves, and drop the masks we are wearing—in short, when we let down our defences. This requirement has also been described as the 'letting-go', which means not merely a partial process but a complete letting-go, even of oneself. For as long as there is the slightest residue left of an individual will—the individual working out a purpose of his own, which is merely a projection from his own mind—God or Reality will not come to him. I would like to quote in this connection, the words of a man who knows by experience:—

'We don't see that only in ending can there be renewal,

the creative, the unknown—not in carrying over from day to day our experiences, our memories and misfortunes. It is only when we die each day to all that is old that there can be the new. The new cannot be where there is continuity— the new being the creative, the unknown, the eternal, God or what you will. The person, the continuous entity, who seeks the unknown, the real, the eternal, will never find it, because he can find only that which he projects out of himself and that which he projects is not the real. Only in ending, in dying, can the new be known; and the man who seeks to find a relationship between life and death, to bridge the continuous with that which he thinks is beyond, is living in a fictitious, unreal world, which is a projection of himself.

'Now is it possible, while living, to die—which means coming to an end, being as nothing? Is it possible, while living in this world where everything is becoming more and more or becoming less and less, where everything is a process of climbing, achieving, succeeding, is it possible, in such a world, to know death? Is it possible to end all memories—not the memory of facts, the way to your house and so on, but the inward attachment through memory to psychological security, the memories that one has accumulated, stored up, and in which one seeks security, happiness? Is it possible to put an end to all that—which means dying every day so that there may be a renewal tomorrow? It is only then that one knows death while living. Only in that dying, in that coming to an end, putting an end to continuity, is there renewal, that creation which is eternal.'*

In essence all religions point to this same truth. In Christian terminology this is: 'Not *my* will but *thine* be done' (Luke 22 : 42). Ramakrishna said: 'When the ego dies, all troubles cease'. But where other religions simply point out the final goal, the desirable end result so to say—and for the rest leave it to an Authority or an Entity outside ourselves to deliver us—Buddhism brings us to the path and gives us a start by telling us that we have to work diligently for our own salvation. Incidentally, later, as we attain more understanding we realize that this 'work' is actually 'no-work', that is, if we qualify the latter term by stating that here 'work' shall

* Krishnamurti, *The First and Last Freedom*, p. 236.

not mean perception, understanding, which is an involuntary
act of pure intellect. This implies not that one 'does' anything in particular in one's inner life but on the contrary
that one no longer wishes to modify it in any way, 'do anything about it'. This is what we have referred to earlier as
the complete 'letting-go' process.

The invaluable service that Buddhism renders can be said,
therefore, to be the fact that it gives us a start—and the Four
Noble Truths do exactly that—by making us realize the
transience of all things and the emptiness of our self nature.
It is however—and this must be emphasized—only a start,
a pointing-out of the path; and after that we are very much
on our own.

Could anyone else effect this essential transformation
in us, the dissolving of attachment to the self? Is a mere
reading of the scriptures sufficient to effect this? Of course
not. You cannot find truth through anybody else; truth is
not static, it is not knowledge, not a formula—it cannot be
written down. If it is, or fixed in any other form, it is no
longer truth.

The question is often asked whether Buddhism is a religion
or a philosophy. Some have called it not a religion but a
therapy, and perhaps—if we insist on giving it a label—this
is the neatest term for it. Now let us look into the meaning
of this; how exactly does it act as a therapy?

Supposing you are ill and the doctor diagnoses your illness
and prescribes a medicine; after taking this more or less
regularly you eventually recover from your illness. The
question now arises: Was it the doctor who cured you
through his medicine? Indirectly yes, but directly and in
actual fact, neither the doctor nor his remedy cured you.
They only prepared the way for something inside you to
regain normality—and without that mysterious 'something'
—which, by the way, doctors call the 'vis medicatrix'—even
a dozen doctors and the combined resources of several phar-
macopœias would be powerless. In final analysis, it is Nature
inside you that has cured you and the 'therapy' simply pro-
vided the most favourable conditions for Nature to take
its course.

Similarly Buddhism is a therapy in the sense that it only
prepares the way for something inside you to start ticking

over in the right way. It seeks to remove the obstacles that stand in the way and it does this in the first place by *making these obstacles known to us*; or, in other words, by removing *avidya*, ignorance. That in short, is the whole therapy, the essence of the Zen approach to Self-Realization. Incidentally, I did not use the term 'enlightenment' just there because I think it might be somewhat misleading. Nothing new is given or added on to us; it is rather an awakening of what has always been there, of what has been part of us if only in a dormant state. From this point of view, I agree with Alan Watts that it would be much better if we adopted the term 'awakening'—a word which has fewer misleading associations.

From the foregoing we have seen, therefore, that Zen works through its negative approach, through No-Work: it teaches through No-Teaching; for by No-Work it enables the You which is Not-You to do all the work, or, to put it more simply, to 'work itself out'. One could also say that it acts like a catalyst, which by definition is a substance that by its mere presence can effect a rapid transformation without being itself affected by that transformation. Our existing vocabulary is hardly adequate for our purpose here but the useful expression 'the You which is Not-You' I have taken from a book entitled *A Theory of Disease* by A. Guirdham, an excellent work that partly covers the same ground but emphasizes more the viewpoint of the pathologist. Since the term in question may not yet be quite clear I shall quote Guirdham for further elucidation. He writes (p. 170):—

'The personality, in pursuing its ambitions and desires, directs itself towards the future and manipulates its desires in accordance with its experience of the past. The You which is Not You is timeless, ambitionless and without desire. It is the undifferentiated and fundamental life within us which has not been entirely malformed and riveted by the iron domination of personality. It is part of the universal consciousness still exempt from the enchainment in the self-consciousness which is a special attribute of each separate personality.

'While the existence of such a substratum of being is not allowed for in current psychology it has been recognized from time immemorial in the sphere of religion. Those who have studied the records of religious experience, which is something totally distinct from the study of the intricate gymnastics of theology, will recognize that my concept of the You which is Not You is similar to that of the real Self as envisaged by the writers on mysticism.

'The uncovering of this real Self, or You which is Not You, in the course of religious experience, meditation with self-analysis or in one or other form of enlightenment, is essentially different from the so-called self-realization which occurs in the process of psycho-analysis. The latter aims at freeing the patient from conflicts occurring between the dynamic and social personalities and from the repression exerted on the former by the latter. The amended self produced by psychoanalysis is essentially the self arising from a new balance of power between these two strata of consciousness.

'The You which is Not You is a form of godhead, imprisoned in our manhood. It is a whisper from the Absolute heard only faintly and infrequently because of the clamour of our personality in pursuit of its private aims.'

In those who are interested in the Way and have an urge for Self-Realization—and even in those who think they have progressed considerably along that Way, there is and will be right till the end when satori is experienced—a continuous tug-of-war going on: a fine balance between the assertive side which always says Yes to the World—and the negative side that works towards the final extinction of the self. It is basically the same process which we see taking place in any society of people—Society being only a projection of individual minds: a balance between material and spiritual forces. Where the equilibrium will lie for a particular individual is entirely a matter of his sensitivity.

With most people who have attained a certain position in the world, perhaps own a house, a car, etc., and enjoy a certain amount of respectability or possibly even esteem— as long as everything goes all right—these assets are all that matter to them. For such a person the equilibrium lies right over on the positive side which affirms him as an individual. The general unsatisfactoriness of life (*dukkha*) is not strongly felt by him for it is drowned in self-expansion; and obviously he will not be the slightest bit interested in any kind of religion—other than as a form of insurance to perpetuate his present pleasant circumstances. Needless to say he will never be able to experience the reality which lies behind the words 'spiritual life', without a complete re-orientation of his thinking, feeling and acting.

For others who are not so completely satisfied with their lives, the equilibrium will continually swing between their positive and negative centres—according to their sensitivity at each moment. In this process we cannot directly interfere because this process is us and that which would interfere can only be our assertive side. All we can hope to do is to take some of the obstacles away—the obstacles which have been indicated to us by men who have already found enlightenment.

Now it may be asked, how is it that in this fine balance between the two opposing factions in us, there is any hope at all that without external interference the balance may swing out decisively towards satori. Why should things settle themselves in the desired direction? The answer is that the natural tendency is always for the greater to overcome the smaller. The Not-Self is the greater—in fact, the self is based on it, being an artefact, a construction of the mind and therefore not grounded in Reality. If the true nature of the assertive side is recognized—or as we have said earlier— if the obstacles become known to us, they lose their significance and eventually vanish altogether. For they never had any independent existence but were brought to life by our faulty vision.

In final analysis, we see therefore that Zen produces clearer perception, deeper insight in our nature not by meddling with it or disciplining it, but by watching quietly and with the greatest alertness. When we do this we engage in true meditation, which is the process of getting to know and completely understand ourselves, and therefore the only means of liberation from our 'selves'. This meditation requires no retirement and no set period of time—on the contrary, it can be very effective in the hustle and bustle of everyday life; it may become, as it were, 'second nature' throughout the greater part of our waking life—and later, we shall find that it operates even in our dream life.

This is also the meaning of Krishnamurti's advice when he says: 'In order to understand yourself you should experiment and observe yourself in your relationship with people and ideas.' Further, he makes it clear that the experiments would have to be carried out by non-doing rather than by doing, by no-thought rather than by thought, for he tells us to stay with our mental states—our fear, sadness, pain, etc.—and not to push them away, try to run away from them or explain them away. We should go deeper into them through passive awareness, which is extreme receptivity, from moment to moment, without accumulating the experience which awareness brings. Finally, a state of creativeness comes about when the self, which is the process of recognition and accumulation, has been completely understood, and so ceases to be.

It is correct to say, I think, that the average person is possessed, enslaved, not only by his possessions but worse still: by his thoughts and emotions. He considers himself far superior to any mechanical control device, such as an electronic brain, because he imagines he is free in his thinking and the electronic brain is not because it is dependent upon the way it has been programmed. Now I maintain that for the ordinary person this is an absolute fallacy, for he, too, is programmed, viz., by the conditioning of the whole of his life to date; such a person, when meeting with certain stimuli from the outside world, will react in an entirely automatic fashion—governed by the reasoning of his ego. This 'reasoning' may at times be so well camouflaged that it may appear to be Pure Reason; psychologists are well acquainted with this phenomenon and call it 'rationalization'. If we had all the data about such a person's mental state at our disposal, his behaviour would be entirely predictable and we would then see that from the beginning he never had the slightest amount of inner freedom and independence, but that all his actions have been entirely governed by the requirements of the 'I', or in a broader sense of the word, upon desire in one form or another—and that therefore all his 'actions' were in reality 'reactions'.

What Zen is really all about, is to free us absolutely from

this enslavement. It does so by destroying, not the emotions but the emotive state—which is a different thing. In the emotive state there is no let-up from the domination of a particular emotional mood which colours all our thoughts and actions, be it a mood of gloom or even of elation—it is a state in which our assertive side is victorious. (It is this, of course, which gives us continuity as a psychological entity —in other words, the upkeep of the ego.) When there is mindfulness it has this peculiar effect that by accepting the emotions one by one as they come along, evaluating them for what they are: manifestations of the little 'I' and there-fore completely irrelevant from any other viewpoint—by just 'looking at' them in this way they are rendered harmless, resulting first in a saner balance between the self and the not-self—and eventually in the complete dissolving away of the self.

From a physiological and cybernetic point of view we may say that the thalamus—which is the centre of the emotions—is made subservient to the cortex rather than vice versa. Nerve impulses on their way from the sense organs to the cortex pass through the thalamus where they give rise to the emotions. Through mindfulness there is a continuous feed-back from the cortex to the thalamus, thus neutralizing the latter's action. After mindfulness has been operating for some time, one finds gradually one's subconscious 'emptying out', the mind becomes more restful and less agitated, the emotions and the imagination become less powerful, making fewer demands, and eventually shrink to negligible pro-portions. When this has taken place the spiritual life may be said to have become actuality, and thereafter the individual finds a spiritual confidence growing in him.

Now this mindfulness, this quiet watching without judgment, which requires in the first place a certain tran-quillity of mind, may sound simple but is a most difficult thing for the mind to come to. For we are so accustomed to doing —to 'getting things done' as we call it—that not to act, to let go completely and observe passively every thought, feeling and emotion seems almost superhuman. But it may become somewhat easier if we really see clearly, and under-stand completely, that any conscious action towards satori must always result in a movement away from satori; for that which acts from the mind always comes from the centre of the self—and therefore strengthens the assertive side which stands in opposition to satori. This is the paradox of Zen: the harder we try to have it, the less likely we are to obtain it; it is like pursuing our own shadow: the faster we run to catch it the faster it moves away. It must be clear, therefore, that Zen could not possibly work through any other means than through No-Work—and that the Way is in reality No-Way since there is no Path to enlightenment: where we are going is where we have always been. In E. Herrigel's book *Zen in the Art of Archery* it is related how the Master never gave any proper teachings in archery but taught in some mysterious negative way very baffling to the unenlightened. The author of this work finally succeeded in shooting his arrows by some kind of non-action—which remained inexplicable even to himself.

This very fundamental insight into the nature of the paradox of Zen is probably the most important single factor and the first step forward on this Way which is No-Way. We find it mirrored in the sayings of various Zen Masters, of which I would like to quote just a few here:—'There is no place in Buddhism for using effort. Just be ordinary and nothing special.'—Lin-chi.[1] The same Master also said: 'To *seek* the Buddha and to *seek* the Dharma is precisely making karma for the hells.'[2]

'Saunter along and stop worrying,
If your thoughts are tied you spoil what is genuine.
. . . . .
The wise person does not strive (*wu-wei*)
The ignorant man ties himself up . . .
If you work on your mind with your mind,
How can you avoid an immense confusion?'—Seng-ts'an.[3]

'My teaching which has come down from the ancient Buddhas is not dependent on meditation or on diligent application of any kind. When you attain the insight as attained by the Buddha, you realize that Mind is Buddha and Buddha is Mind, that Mind, Buddha, sentient beings, Bodhi (enlightenment) and Klesa (passions) are one and the same substance, while they vary in names.'—Shih-tou.[4] The negative message of Zen is also well expressed by a simple and rather terse definition of Zen:—

> 'No thought, no reflection, no analysis,
> No cultivation, no intention;
> Let it settle itself.' (The six precepts of Tilopa)[5]

This, it seems to me, sums it up beautifully and also mentions the various obstacles such as thought, grasping, etc.—in short the ceaseless activities of the mind which have to come to an end before 'it' can settle 'itself'. The whole Zen 'training' is in essence not a direct training to satori but only indirectly so; for it is direct only in a negative way: the clearing away of the hindrances that stand in the way of enlightenment. The greatest hindrance, it may be said, to your achieving satori is, therefore, You, the self—since all hindrances spring from that source, which always tries to strengthen itself—by virtue of being the self—and therefore always interferes with the workings of the Not-Self in which your being is grounded.

No fundamental transformation can take place if it is not absolutely clear that all the mind's activities and strivings are engendered by the Ego—this Ego that is in itself an artificial construction of the mind, which has no reality but in our mind—and that there is nothing else but this Ego that stands between us and absolute happiness and freedom. But then it must also be evident that satori, which occurs when this vicious circle and with it, the Ego, is broken, is not as some people seem to think, final Victory—after which we really are somebody—but on the contrary complete and final Defeat—the silencing forever of the assertive side of our being, the becoming like Nothing . . . The individual then sees for the first time the world from an Absolute point of view, and ceases to be at odds with his own humanity.

In the process that leads to the elimination of the self, which may take place when things are left to work themselves out, an important factor can most certainly be the experience of humiliation.

This particular experience, which the ordinary person feels as humiliation is, when undergone by the enlightened person, no longer felt as such because there is no longer any

'I'-consciousness to be affected. The degree to which humiliation is still experienced as a pain is an indication of the
strength of the self. Another important point is that to the
unenlightened person who is sincere in his attitude towards
the Way, humiliation can be an experience which may assist
greatly in the process of awakening. This is probably the real
meaning of Suffering that through it we may find a Way to
overcome this Suffering and come face to face with Reality.

The same principle of the potential beneficial effects of
humiliation seems to me to be the deeper meaning of some of
the strange goings-on in Zen monasteries. We often read of a
student, in search of the highest truth, being relegated to
kitchen duties or other menial occupations; and perhaps
when approaching the Master for instruction being told: 'go
and wash your bowls'—or something like that. This may
strike us as somewhat rough—or even comical—but then we
have to remember again that Zen-teaching operates through
No-Teaching and that only the Master is in a position to judge
what is best for each particular student. Also, in this way,
the student may discover for himself that the spiritual life
does not lie away from the ordinary everyday existence, and
that it may be attained by being perfectly ordinary and doing
nothing special.

Another Zen-practice which may seem quite puzzling in
Western eyes is that of the beating by the Master. But here,
we must admit that as soon as we hear about this our reaction is coloured by our previous conditioning—our notions
of good and bad. In Zen, no such considerations exist but the
only criterion is the means to an end, the *upaya* of Buddhism
(meaning roughly 'skilful means')—the end in this case
being the earliest possible awakening of the student. The
rough handling, the thirty blows, etc., seem to me to have a
twofold significance: in the first place, they may assist the
student by making him sharply aware of his 'I'-consciousness
—in order that he may eventually transcend it; and in the
second place from the reaction of the student the Master
will get a very good idea of the former's state of mind and
of his progress towards satori. And I would not be at all
surprised if a third, more subtle factor were operating as
well: the possibility of a sudden awakening by a mechanism

perhaps somewhat similar to that employed when we slap an hysteric in the face in order to awaken him from his delusional dreaming.

[1] A. W. Watts, *The Way of Zen*, p. 101.
[2] *Ibid.*, p. 102.
[3] *Ibid.*, p. 89.
[4] D. T. Suzuki, *Manual of Zen Buddhism*, London, Rider, 1956, p. 105.
[5] Watts, op. cit., p. 79.

15

IS ZEN FOR THE WEST?

There are Buddhists in the West who would like nothing better than to import Japanese Zen lock, stock and barrel—with its monasteries, koan techniques, etc. This, I think, would not only amount to the height of absurdity but would go directly against the whole spirit of Zen. Zen is not static but flexible and expresses itself in different forms according to time, place and circumstances. The important point is that Zen grew to its present form in Japan as part and parcel of Japanese culture and within this cultural framework developed as an historical necessity.

The principle of Zen being, 'Let it settle itself—without external moulding, or cultivation', Zen must and, I think, will settle itself also in the West and when left to do so grow into a form which will be found to be hundred per cent. appropriate to our cultural and historical background.

The essential thing to realize, however, is that in final analysis it is only the Zen *experience* that counts—the approach and the experience are still worlds apart. The former is confined within the limits of conceptual thinking and as such liable to argument, to opinion—the experience, however, is beyond the level of concepts and independent of space and time. Consequently there is always a danger that the 'preparation' of the mind, the awakening of intelligence, which aims only at clearing away the obstacles to the experience, is taken as an end in itself with the result that one obstacle has only been replaced by another. In Zen terminology this is described as taking the finger which points to the Moon for the Moon.

We see this sort of pitfall clearly exemplified in certain types of Yoga: one may read in Yoga literature, for example, that the carrying out of certain exercises—breathing,

meditating in a particular posture and what not—is all that
is required and bound to lead to enlightenment in the end
if only pursued long enough. In actual fact all these conscious efforts of the mind to 'get' enlightenment may well
form the greatest hindrance to that experience. The im-
portation of Japanese techniques without more ado is almost
certain to lead to just such a situation. Once this damage is
done and Zen has become just another cult amongst many,
we may wish we had never heard of Japanese Zen methods.

We must face the fact that it is unfortunately not possible
to 'teach' anybody to have the Zen experience. It is, however, possible to point out some of the most formidable
obstacles which stand in the way to that experience, particularly for us in the West. In the main they are the
following three:—

There is first the general idea of gain in people's minds as
when on first hearing of Zen they immediately ask 'what do
I get out of it?' In other words, even Zen should serve them
in the process of becoming; in looking for a purpose in the
future and thereby escaping from what *is* here and now. It
is this everlasting striving for fulfilment, to make purposeful
that which is purposeless by setting up some goal which has
to be attained at all costs, and for which end we are even
prepared to kill one another—it is this continuous struggle
that has fostered the delusion of the 'me' and the 'mine' and
brought about the effective isolation of the individual. The
process has been operative particularly in the West where
competition for material wealth has always been extremely
severe, especially since the time of the Industrial Revolution.

A second obstacle is the tendency to question everything
according to a moral yardstick: something is either good, or
it is evil, virtuous or wicked. The desire for such facile classi-
fication is in actual fact based on an undercurrent of
righteousness—which is only another form of covering up
our feeling of emptiness, of nothingness—that is, the expression of a kind of moral inferiority complex.

And third, there is the dualistic notion of body and mind,
mind and matter, which—as Easterners see it—is the malady
of the West: we are all suffering from this schizophrenia.
Following from this we often have arguments as to which
is better; the Christian attitude of looking outward or the

Buddhist attitude of looking inward. But in reality there is no problem here: there is no difference between outward and inward—this is all a delusion based upon 'thinking', i.e. putting 'things' in a space-time framework of reference and upon the fallacious dualistic notion of body versus mind.

PART TWO

16

WHY BUDDHISM?

Recently at a lecture held at the Buddhist Society in London someone asked a very pertinent and fundamental question: 'Why should one take up Buddhism?' Apart from the fact that the question was wrongly formulated through ignorance about Buddhism (and the questioner could not be blamed for this), it was not adequately answered; now it seems to me that it deserved a better fate, and not only because of the obvious challenge it presents to the Buddhist.

If I were to answer this question I would begin by pointing out that one does not 'take up' Buddhism—as though it were another kind of leisure activity. One 'is taken up' by Buddhism, or one is not—this is what actually happens. The question should therefore be: 'What is the significance of being taken up by Buddhism?' Let us look at the problem in this form.

Many people see in Buddhism a way of reducing suffering and nothing more. Now, if the Buddhist case rested solely on being able to alleviate the amount of suffering in this world, it would be enormous; but it would still only be some kind of super-anaesthetic. And perhaps it could not then be considered of universal value, for some would say: 'I am quite happy the way I am, I feel I do not 'suffer', or not all that much, for having to bother with Buddhism' (and this objection would be unanswerable!).

The real position is entirely different. The relief of suffering and the creation of happiness are never ends in themselves; indeed, where they have become ends in themselves they constitute effective hindrances to enlightenment. Happiness is the result of Reality, it is incidental to the attainment of the Goal. The answer which our friend should have been given is something like this: What is called

Buddhism is nothing but an extended vision of life, a deeper understanding of Reality, which can lead to a state of being which is as different from the ordinary life as is our waking state from sleep. In this new life there is direct insight into the nature of things, complete intelligence and freedom, bliss and love. Once ignorance and dualistic thinking have been cleared away by one's own mental maturing process, one automatically treads the path of Buddhism, whether one is aware of this or not. Then, whether or not one calls oneself a Buddhist is no longer of any importance.

17

COMMON SENSE AND BUDDHISM

It seems to me that whatever approach is followed, whether that of common sense (which is basically that of science), or of Buddhism, or psychology—to the seeker of Truth all roads lead eventually to a point of view, an 'insight', which Zen followers would call 'Zen'; others (who may never have heard the word) would possibly call it something else, or perhaps not feel any need to name it at all. It is, I think, rather important for Buddhists in general and for Zen 'followers' in particular to recognize that there are also other people, who have arrived at the same fundamental insights without having gone through a formal study of Zen writings or Buddhist scriptures. Some of these people may well be all the better for it in their understanding, for was it not Alan Watts who wrote in one of his books that in order to approach Zen most successfully one should first forget everything one has learned, even one's knowledge of Buddhism.

To many people the way of Zen does not seem to 'make sense' at all—to them it is the opposite of any common sense approach. So in this connection it may not be out of place first to consider the question of common sense *versus* non-sense. It seems to me that the two need not necessarily stand in opposition to each other. Very often whether something strikes us as non-sense or as common sense is determined by our degree of familiarity with it; as our familiarity with a new concept increases, our point of view shifts and our outlook broadens. There are many examples from the development of knowledge through the ages where new concepts were first received as complete non-sense, later became promoted to common sense, at the same time that the old superseded concepts were demoted from common sense to non-sense.

For example, before Copernicus anybody who maintained that the earth was revolving around the sun was talking nonsense and the prevalent view that the sun revolved around a stationary earth was common sense—too demonstrably true to need doubting. Today, anybody who maintains the latter view would be regarded as a crank. 'After all, the earth is one of the sun's planets and therefore it is quite plain that she revolves around the sun'—such would be one's natural reaction. (In other words we have been properly conditioned to the new concept). This instance shows clearly the relativity, as it were, of common sense and non-sense, being entirely based upon existing familiarity or unfamiliarity with a particular concept.

Many other examples can be given from the history of science showing that new concepts were initially regarded as complete non-sense, followed—after a period of familiarization—by a complete reversal in assessment. Of these only the following instances will be mentioned: the concept of spontaneous generation before and after Pasteur; inconvertibility of mass and energy before and after Einstein propounded his famous equation $E=mc^2$ (and as far as the general public are concerned: before and after the atomic bomb); and the summation of velocities before and after the relativity theory (we shall refer to this later; see p. 105).

It is only the genius or the man far ahead of his time for whom non-sense is often common sense, serving him as a point of departure for his thinking.

At the same time common sense has often produced a certain complacency and acted as a brake on the spirit of enquiry. There is an utterance by E. T. Bell on this point that runs as follows: 'That is precisely what common sense is for, to be jarred into uncommon sense. One of the chief services which mathematics has rendered the human race in the past century is to put "common sense" where it belongs, on the topmost shelf next to the dusty canister labelled "discarded nonsense".'*

However, we must not fall into the error of judging one superior to the other. Ultimately both common sense and non-sense—being a pair of opposites—have to be trans-

* As recorded in A. Korzybski's *Science and Sanity*; see also the remarks made about mathematics on p. 118 of the present work.

cended. And what then is the result? *Sense!*, but in the sense of sense-impression; or the *consciousness of momentary observation* prior to interpretation through memory—and therefore still free from any conditioning influence which immediately classifies the experience as either common or non-sense.

I have dwelt on this subject rather long because it may help in our understanding of Zen, where the insights acquired when translated into words and concepts often strike us as contradictory to the experiences of the everyday world—in short, Zen has been said to be identical with some special form of nonsense.

Next I would like to consider for a moment another important aspect of Zen: it is said to lead to paradoxes. But it is not only Zen that thrives on paradox; so does science! The following two examples may suffice to illustrate this. Science tells us that were we to invent a super-rocket with infinitely large thrust there would still be a maximum velocity which would limit our journey through space (namely the velocity of light). This would mean then that apparent nothingness can hold us back in some way— signifying either that nothingness, empty space, is not quite that—or that perhaps we and our spaceship are essentially of the nature of nothingness, or most probably: that both are true.

A second example of the paradox in science is the following: Take the smallest particle of matter known to science: an electron. This 'entity' will as it were explode under close observation for it cannot be pinpointed in space and time! Furthermore, although it possesses mass, it does not behave purely in the way we would expect of a material corpuscle, for it also manifests itself as an electromagnetic radiation.

Now all this may be thought to be somewhat irrelevant to the subject of Buddhism, but this, I think, is not so, for Buddhism is concerned with Reality in all its manifestations. It can, in fact, be highly instructive if we regard these examples as a new type of 'koan'. We shall see, then, that what makes the new concepts appear nonsensical, and sometimes paradoxical, is the different and unexpected point of view from which the problem is approached. For centuries man had identified himself with the earth as being the centre of the Universe: the latter was considered as something external, something separate.

The end of this epoch came with Copernicus, whose new concept set going a revolution in the thinking of his contemporaries—*because it compelled them to look at the world from a different viewpoint.* The development of science from there on indicates a broadening of thinking, in which the part of the human observer became—to put it loosely— ever less absolute and more relative.

A similar thing we can observe when a man begins to take notice of Zen (or perhaps more accurately: when Zen begins to take notice of him!). All his familiar notions drop away and the new insights acquired seem, superficially, contradictory to everyday experience. But perhaps we can now find the reason for this, and why also Zen should lead us to a paradoxical view of the world. To this end we should ask ourselves the question: Can we detect whether there lies at the basis of the Zen experience an unexpected shift of viewpoint, a new frame of reference to encompass the phenomenal world? If we can, then perhaps it may considerably smooth our way along the actual path of Zen.

In trying to answer this question we should first of all see that in Zen the development of knowledge, as sketched previously, has gone one step further still—and has become even more relative than in science. That is to say, in satori the stage would be reached that the ultimum of self-knowledge has been attained leading to complete liberation from the self. To the man who has this experience, for the first time in his life knowledge of the Universe is no longer just 'knowledge' which he has acquired, but a complete realization of the meaning, of the essential nature of such knowledge. This realization is therefore no longer on a par with knowledge: it is knowledge transcended, or in Zen terminology 'No-knowledge'. In such a man satori has led to the transcending of all duality, of the subject-object relationship, of the 'I' viewing the world.

And so we have now arrived at a rather unexpected answer to the question as to a possible shift of viewpoint in Zen: 'There is no point of view in Zen, and there is no Zen point of view which is communicable to others; things are somehow seen in their totality.' One could also say that the

Zen 'point of view' does not consist in a certain angle of vision, but comprises all possible angles. Now we can perhaps understand why Zen is also called the 'doctrine of no-mind': because thought and knowledge are dualistic, based on symbols for reality—in fact, on abstractions. The point is that *knowledge about* is always a relationship between the knower and the known—or between subject and object. But where we have a subject and an object we have defined the limits of both these 'entities'—in other words, we have made abstractions because the defining of limits is an arbitrary and mind-made process.

18

ON NON-DUALITY

To come to the insight of non-duality—and we are here touching as it were on the heart of the matter, so essential to an understanding of the Zen way—it may be useful to deal at length with an approach to epistemology, i.e. a theory of knowledge, which fits in with the facts of science and, as will be shown, inevitably leads to the Zen position. In the course of this analysis I shall intentionally deviate here and there in order to deal with several problems that may appear to be only side issues, but which can actually all contribute to clarifying the main issue.

'Cognition' or the act of knowing seems to imply a relationship between an observer and an object. So first of all let us look into the nature of the observer in order to understand the total process. The observer obviously consists of some sensing apparatus, viz., the five senses, plus an 'interpreter', or 'data analyser': the brain, the thought-machine. The former, the sensing apparatus comprising the five senses, has its physical counterparts in man-made scientific instruments, and although the natural products are in many ways infinitely more refined, their essential nature is similar to or identical with that of the artefacts and their workings are relatively well understood so that they do not merit any further discussion here.

Let us therefore now look into the nature and the workings of the human thought-machine.

In considering then the nature of this thought-machine, we are faced with the problem of the 'self'. The information which is fed in through the sense organs is in some way co-ordinated and interpreted by—we should be inclined to say—by a 'something', a discriminating centre, our 'consciousness'. But is it a 'thing', i.e. a well-defined entity which is limited in space and time? Since everything else, every object and every phenomenon we observe presents itself in space and time, we tend to assume the same of consciousness. We are inclined to say with Descartes: there is thought, consciousness; therefore that which produces or manifests this consciousness must be a separate, permanent entity, the 'I' or the self—that if we have to doubt everything else we can at least be certain this 'I' exists as an indisputable fact.

But is not this begging the question, or perhaps wishful thinking ensuing from clinging to a straw of permanency in a transient world, a world in which as has been made clear by Sunyavada or Madhyamika—which is the basic metaphysical system that underlies Buddhism and was mainly developed by Nagarjuna—all objects and phenomena are unreal in the sense that they are indeterminate. This is a point which is often misunderstood by people who designate this philosophy as a useless form of dialectic, or as pure nihilism. Sunyavada does not deny the reality of the phenomenal world—it only clearly and carefully distinguishes between Reality and its Manifestation. The phenomenal world is reality in so far as it is the manifestation of that Reality—it is unreal in so far as it is defined or determined in terms of phenomenal events, since like cannot be defined by like but only by something more fundamental than itself—in other words: any 'concept' about the phenomenal world is hollow, unreal.* Thus there remains only to see things purely in their 'suchness'.

The human attitude towards this problem is at once highly interesting and complex. Subconsciously man realizes the emptiness of all objects and objectives in this world—the complete 'futility' of it all as he will sometimes put it. However, having been wrongly educated in this matter and been conditioned to base his whole life on the so-called achievement of certain objectives without which life would have no 'value', a serious conflict is ever present in his subconscious: an inevitable result of a fundamental contradiction. This subtle form of neurosis expresses itself in the affirmation of the ego as a distinct entity, in a so-called positive attitude

* For a fuller discussion of Madhyamika I refer to Prof. T.R.V. Murti's excellent work: *The Central Philosophy of Buddhism*, London, Allen & Unwin, 1961, 2nd edn.

towards life which is the covering-up of this profound aching feeling of despair and 'emptiness'.

According to Zen the 'seeing into one's own nature' is the complete realization of this emptiness of the phenomenal world, of multiplicity, and of the self. By means of this intensely penetrating perception into things-as-they-really-are, conceptualized thinking is transcended and—as Buddhists say—Buddhahood attained—that is, Reality undergone as a direct experience. The ego as a separate entity is then seen as a delusion and the source of all attachments, desires and suffering. The feeling of futility and despair in man before satori is then also seen as unreal and entirely the result of a conditioning process which was not based on reality but on the imaginative-emotional activity of the mind.

But I have deviated, since I have gone into the reasons why man persists in certain mistaken notions. Now let us continue our investigation into the correctness or otherwise of the usual dualistic notion of consciousness. Man is so wont to consider mind and body as two different entities that he entertains the notion that consciousness 'dwells' in the body —or perhaps more specifically in some part of the body like the head, or the heart (I think it is the Polynesians who consider the heart as the centre of consciousness).

Consequently he claims existence as a distinctly defined ego when he contends that his body and his mind are uniquely 'his'. Now there are several logical errors and unproven assumptions underlying this thought process, which is therefore really more in the nature of a 'jumping to conclusions'. In the first place there are the unwritten assumptions that body and mind are separate, and that as separate things they manifest themselves similarly, that is, since body has form, so must also mind have a form; the two forms must somehow fit together or possibly coincide; there must be some third entity that joins both forms together; the total aggregate of mind in body is an island in the universe totally isolated from any other such island—this is said to constitute individuality or personality. Furthermore, each such aggregate is an enduring composite—at least until the physical death of the body—which somehow seems to defy the ubiquitous transience that may be observed in the

Universe—all this is said to constitute the 'self' or the 'ego' and to be regarded not as an empirical composite but as a facet of Absolute Reality.

To the person who has not made these various arbitrary and unwarranted assumptions some of which have been mentioned here, the dualistic outlook is quite plainly unreal, and he simply cannot help viewing the world in a non-dualistic manner. To that person mind and body would still appear as mind and body but with this difference that the implied metaphysical speculation of their inter-relationship and their location in space and time would be totally absent. Mind and body would be regarded as two manifestations of the reality which lies behind the phenomenal world, and which is one; in other words: body equals mind, if we feel inclined to present it in a mathematical form.

The non-dualist would then go one step further and say: that one reality which transcends my body and mind is no different from the One Reality that underlies all the phenomenal world; that one reality which appears as 'me' is part of the great stream of Life that not only encompasses organic life but also the inanimate world—that stream, which because it is ever in a flux, represents transience itself. To see it in any other way would require another set of arbitrary and unwarranted assumptions on perception of Reality, but to the Zen person these words no longer stand for an intellectual proposition but are the translation of a vivid experience into language.

Now it may be possible to prove on purely logical grounds that the dualistic position is completely untenable (and this, I think, has already been done by the powerful dialectic of Nagarjuna and those who came after him); to prove by the same means that non-dualism is correct may be very difficult, in fact, I consider it impossible. This must be so for two reasons: it is not a matter of two alternatives of which when one is proved wrong the other must necessarily be right. Nagarjuna simply shows that any conceptualized view on reality is necessarily hollow—and he does not deny that the same applies to his own dialectic; but he shows that this does not invalidate, but actually confirms his thesis.*

In the second place the mere fact of showing a particular

* See T. R. V. Murti, op. cit.

point by logical argument, by the process of Reason, is by definition dualistic being based on the discursive intellect which itself came about through being firmly based on dualism. So if we tried to use dualism to prove non-dualism this would simply make us look ridiculous. However, what can be done is that discursive reasoning can by its own means show the limits of its capacities and range of applicability. Again, this does not prove anything at all, but its realization has a wonderful effect in increasing one's awareness and perception of reality, and opens the way for Prajna, or Intuition, to develop itself in preparation for the eventual explosion of satori. At the same time, application of the scientific method can often go a long way in showing the plausibility or otherwise of certain commonly held views.

For instance, somebody who has followed my criticism of the usual dualistic way of considering body and mind, may put in the following objection. He may say: I grant you that you have made clear to me that body and mind are one. But far from proving to me that the self is not a distinct entity, you have actually by your own words weakened your case because now I can maintain with all the more reason the separate identity of the self; as a thing in time and space *I am my body*. Since my body appears to be a thing with self-nature, the same must apply to the ego.

How do we deal with such an objection? In actual fact, the position we are asked to refute is very similar to that held by the pure materialist. To the materialist only matter, the body, exists, mind simply being a by-product of the brain, somewhat similar to the way that hormones are produced by the glands with internal secretion. In both cases we have the standpoint that the self is defined in space and time by the body; since the body is a definite 'thing', so must the self be.

The fallacy lies in the former part of the proposition. In the first place the body is a composite, made up of many elements. Biochemists and physiologists have taken out tissues, even complete organs like a heart, and kept these functioning outside the body from which it was taken. Recent reports have it that Russian scientists have been able to transplant vital organs from one individual organism to another. In view of these facts what remains of our conception of individuality? There are many facts in biochemistry that underline the essential unity of all life. Identical biochemical processes occur in different individuals, and from a more general point of view even the uniqueness of the species does not indicate otherwise. The theory of evolution has namely shown that the different species are closely related to each other, and that in fact one species may suddenly produce another by so-called 'mutations', which may be brought about, for example, by particular types of radiation.

The chemical structure of certain enzymes, which are biochemical catalysts, are often very similar in widely divergent branches of life. For example, hæm, the red pigment occurring in blood, is present in all living cells as a component of enzymes concerned in biological oxidations.* It appears to be very similar in chemical composition to chlorophyll, the green colouring matter of plants, the presence of which is necessary for photosynthesis. The main difference between the two is that the former contains iron, the latter magnesium in an otherwise nearly identical framework consisting of carbon, hydrogen, nitrogen and oxygen atoms. Looking objectively at all these data supplied by the physical and biological sciences a grand vista of Life as one great and extremely complicated jig-saw puzzle becomes inevitable. A vista, however, that does not only comprise life but also the inanimate world since throughout the Universe the same physical elements occur, and the same physical laws govern their interrelationships.

And lastly in this context, a few words must be said about the body having definite spatial extensions. My body is that part of me of which I become aware through the senses. Owing to my sense of sight my body appears to me as a definite thing in space—because everything my sight tells me is interpreted spatially. Blind people who suddenly regain their vision do not see things spatially, as this is a function of the brain which is only gradually developed. Therefore, to such people the notion of space as we have it is utterly alien, and they have to learn to see things spatially; i.e. they acquire through conditioning what in the young infant has taken place as a natural concomitant of development.

*A. K. Anderson, *Essentials of Physiological Chemistry*, p. 152.

Furthermore, my skin, which seems to limit me, is in continuous interaction with the atmosphere, contributing to some extent to my general respiration process; it is also absorbing heat energy or releasing it as the case may be, and receiving important data for the senses. Far from being the end of my organic existence, my skin seems to be in the middle of it all, actively participating in metabolic and neurological processes. Unlike the cellophane skin that envelopes the sausage, my skin is not a seal, but a gateway. Everything I do, and even everything that goes on inside my skin, is in some way related, to that which goes on outside; in fact, it would be more correct to say that everything that happens within my organism is part of the greater process of life whose manifestations transcend the delineation of my skin.

Even my independent mobility is in actual fact an illusion: any movement that my body makes is never restricted to my body alone. Strictly speaking what takes place is a disturbance in the balance of forces of mass attraction between different bodies around a common gravitational centre. Because the earth is so large and in comparison my body so small, any movement my body makes will only cause an infinitesimally small movement of the earth—or in other words, our common gravitational centre coincides with the gravitational centre of the earth. But this does not alter the fact that in principle there is *inter*action between the bodies and not merely action. If we imagine the earth to shrink to the dimensions of a small artificial satellite of comparable weight to that of my body, then indeed would all my bodily movements have to be considered as joint and absolutely simultaneous movements of the satellite and me.

Thus far we have looked at things from the macromolecular point of view. From the micromolecular and submolecular points of view there is even greater force behind the argument against duality. Not only do the atoms of my skin, of the whole of my body have electromagnetic fields that, according to classical physics, extend into space as far as infinity (whatever that means!), but the whole notion of spatial dimension collapses here; when we examine some of the very smallest fundamental particles that constitute the atom, we find it is completely meaningless to talk about their location in space and time: they no longer behave as though they were corpuscles, and as the nearest thing to describing them physicists use the term 'waves of probability'. The substratum, however, is unknown, or rather it cannot be conveyed as something that makes sense to the discursive intellect; all we are left with is a mathematical equation, and a four-dimensional one at that.

Now it is important to realize why this situation has come about in physics and that it had to come about. When we go on exploring ever smaller so-called 'fundamental' particles there must come a time that we will break through, what I propose to call the 'space-time barrier', in other words we shall not recognize properties and attributes any longer. Notions such as solidity, mass, energy, etc., cease to have any meaning since these are the properties of the macro- or micro-molecular worlds. In sub-fundamental particle size it will be obviously impossible to go on describing properties in terms of these particles themselves. This would be just as impossible as a knife cutting itself or an eye seeing itself. (See also the remarks made on p. 89 regarding Sunyavada.) Or one can look at it this way: the unknown cannot be expressed in terms of the known. Hence some physicists feel that fundamental particles, e.g. the electron, really stand for 'events', or the momentary manifestations of general processes.

The same seems to apply to physical constants at the other end of the scale of magnitudes, such as the speed of light, which is the maximum speed possible in nature. Just as we could not go on subdividing matter (and thus, space) any further, so any entity travelling through space at the speed of light cannot be further accelerated since no higher velocity is physically possible. This seems to me a similar paradox, a similar case where comprehension and insight come to an end—have to come to an end because once again we impinge on the 'space-time barrier'.

19

HUI-NENG AND BERKELEY

In the previous essay we have seen that in fact the observer as a permanent entity does not exist; at the same time we can see that the 'object' does not really exist as such—by definition the object is something in space and time, but as has already been shown for the 'personality' of the observer, similarly it can be shown that the 'object' has no real existence in space and time but only comes through to us in that particular manifestation. To illustrate once again that the spatial extensions which we assign to a body are purely arbitrary, we can see that contemplating for instance a sphere its 'dimensions' are conditioned by our senses. Were we able to perceive, e.g. the sphere's own gravitational field, the object would become of infinite size. Another example is that of the 'radio-star', which is completely non-existent to our senses, even with the aid of the most powerful telescope, but can be perceived as an object or as some 'thing' by means of a radiotelescope. And similarly, it can be shown that the object has no 'age' or 'duration' apart from our mind—since time also is a result of mind, of thought, and has no independent existence (indeed, once the 'thingness' of an object has been destroyed it becomes meaningless to speak of 'its' age).

It may be interesting in this connection to mention that sometimes science or the intellect in its most penetrating moods, can actually prove and demonstrate by logical means that things are not what they seem to be, hinting that no thing has any self-nature, because its 'attributes' are just as much conditioned by that which lies outside the thing as by the thing itself—this, as we have seen before is Sunyavada, the basic philosophy underlying Buddhism.

For example, in considering the colour red, the average

person thinks of 'redness' as an 'absolute' property of red light waves. Yet it can be proved that this is not so; and that, for example. what is red to one person could be yellow to another—and this, without even postulating colour blindness or inherently different colour perceptions in different observers.

To this end let us again digress for a moment and examine what colour is. Scientists tell us that for example a red light source emits light of a certain wavelength or frequency. White light can be split into different colours, each with a distinct frequency of its own. Therefore colours differ from each other only in respect of this frequency. But if we look into the notion of frequency what do we find? We can roughly define this as the number of wave crests per second reaching the eye; and, obviously, this is where *time* comes in. It must be clear, now, that from the viewpoint of eternity, light is just light, and consequently red=blue and blue= yellow, etc. In other words, colour differentiation is a peculiarity of our mechanism of sense perception that puts everything in a space-time framework.

Just as our thought is fundamentally based on time (without time, memory, there would be no thought) so is our perception of light (and of course, that of sound) based on time. But as in thought, time can be transcended in the realization of the Eternal Now, so also can time be transcended in sense perception by the arrangement of certain well-controlled experiments, even if only in our imagination. Suppose two observers are perceiving an orange light source in space. Both will see orange as long as they are stationary with respect to that light source. But now one observer starts travelling towards it and the other away from it with roughly the same (very high) speed. Since more wave crests per time unit will now hit the eye of the former observer, at a certain travelling speed what appeared to him orange when at rest will now appear yellow to him. Similarly, fewer wave crests per time unit will reach the second observer, and at a certain velocity the 'orange' will appear red to him. A phenomenon based on this mechanism (but on a very much smaller scale than in our imaginary experiment) is actually observable in nature and is called 'Doppler effect'.

It is imaginary experiments and considerations such as

these which may possibly assist us in grasping the meaning of Sunyavada, or the essential emptiness of the world of space and time in which we experience.

As a result of our examination we are therefore forced to the conclusion that were it not for our mind, for our thoughts, the 'object' would have no real existence in the sense which these words usually convey. We have thus also come to understand more fully the first proclamation made by the Sixth Patriarch, Hui-neng: 'From the first not a thing is.'

Some readers may be struck by the similarity in conclusion between Hui-neng and the British philosopher George Berkeley (1685-1753). However, Bishop Berkeley's philosophy is only apparently in accord with our findings. He, too, states that but for the perceiver objects do not exist; but when he further writes that since material objects always exist, this necessitates the assumption of a God who always perceives them, he clearly shows that he has missed the point completely and has not attained the same insight as Hui-neng. It is evident, therefore, that Berkeley never succeeded in extricating himself from the morass of dualism; his error is due to the confounding of two levels of reality: phenomenal manifestations and the absolute underlying reality. When Hui-neng declares that from the first not a thing is, the emphasis lies on 'thing' and so he refers only to the phenomenal world. Berkeley, on the other hand, sees only the choice theism or nihilism.

At the same time as it is realized that from the first not a thing is, the fact that conversely our mind, our thoughts, would be non-existent without sense-impressions continuously impinging on our sense organs, must not be lost sight of. This leads us to recognize the following remarkable state of affairs: but for the observer, the phenomenal universe does not exist and but for the phenomenal universe the observer does not exist. In other words, both cannot have an *independent* existence at the same time. The head could not exist but for the body and vice versa!

But all this clearly signifies the end of dualism. For assuming the existence of the observer, the 'I', this could not logically *act upon* the universe if the latter is already implicit in the former. The knife that cuts cannot cut itself! Under these circumstances it becomes meaningless to talk about the observer, the self, for by these terms is implied some centre that can act and think independently: the subject-object duality has dissolved like snow in the sun. Any apparent action which the self therefore performs upon the non-self is in actual fact a process allowed by the Absolute, God—or, more accurately, any such action is only one of the manifestations, touching the self, of the Absolute on the temporal plane. Seen in this light, the 'actions' of the self should be called more appropriately 'events', and causality ceases to have any meaning; the latter concept, too, is apparent, and valid only as an abstraction on the phenomenal level of reality. It must be noted here that Nagarjuna in his own way also arrived at the conclusion that cause and effect are merely apparent.

So far our approach has of necessity been developed by using logical concepts and dialectic—in other words, based on dualism. This is the method of mathematics, philosophy and organized religion. Now, having attained the extreme limit of conceptualized thinking, we find ourselves standing on the edge of a precipice beyond which lies the abyss of the Void, of Emptiness, that to us is the Unknown. Surprisingly, we have come to recognize that *the ultimate triumph of intellection is its destruction, or rather its transcendence*. To go any further in our search for Truth, we must throw ourselves over the precipice, there is nothing more to be said; it only befits us to maintain the Noble Silence of the Buddha . . .

20

BIOLOGICAL EVOLUTION AND THE MIND

In the previous essay we have seen that, paradoxically, cognition turns out to be an interdependent relationship of non-existent 'entities'. On a deeper level of reality, what had been designated as a relationship is therefore really a process —like the falling of a leaf from a tree or the movement of the waves in the ocean—a process that does not stand by itself in isolation but is part of the Total World Process that only appears as an infinite number of individual activities or manifestations. Once we have completely understood this, the subject-object relationship has been transcended and duality and plurality cease to have any existentialist significance; they are then seen as the direct results of 'Avidya', of Ignorance.

Zen may be purely regarded as the taking away of this ignorance. It has been likened to a thorn which removes another thorn in the flesh, whereafter both thorns can be thrown away. It could also be said to be like an all-consuming flame that burns away all the rubbish from the mind, thereby removing ignorance and all the evil effects thereof, and finally when it has burned itself out, leaving nothing but stark Reality.

In the present essay I propose to examine the impasse the human situation has got into both from a psychological and a general biological angle. Psychologically, we see that man's mind is in continuous agitation and it is this agitation which acts as a barrier between him and Reality. As Hubert Benoit put it in his book *The Supreme Doctrine* (p. 106): 'Man believes in the utility of his agitation because he does not think that he is anything but that personal "me" which he perceives in the dualistic manner. He does not know that there is in him something quite different from this visible personal "me", something invisible which works in his favour in the dark. Identifying himself with his perceptible phenomena, in particular with his imaginative mind, he does not think that he is anything more.'

Yet, if we look closely at the machinery of our bodies, the idea of a Principle is forced upon us, which continuously acts in us, organizes and co-ordinates a large number of extremely complicated physiological processes. It is not only that this Principle maintains us, but through it we have grown to what we are from an undifferentiated egg cell. It is therefore correct to say that we are the Manifestation of that Principle.

The presence in us of the Principle—which is synonymous with Mind, the Unconscious or Buddhahood (terms more commonly used in Buddhism)—implies the necessity for non-doing. The degree to which we engage in non-doing constitutes the extent of our 'faith'. This situation often confuses outsiders who think that Buddhism is some kind of fatalism. The difficulty lies in the nature of the non-doing, for what is non-doing on one level is doing on another. With the ordinary person who is not aware of his real nature, viz. of being the manifestation of the Principle, his mind functions independently of Mind. Often the former works against the latter, and the individual makes himself ill. With the enlightened person, however, his mind works in harmony with Mind; and to the extent that all his activities come forth naturally and spontaneously from the unfolding of the Principle, his own mind, or self, ceases to exist even as an empirical reality. In Christian terminology this has been expressed by: 'I live, yet not I but Christ liveth in me.'

Far from being fatalism, it may now be appreciated that Zen is on the contrary activity, doing; but it is doing without the doer—and this is called 'non-doing'.

Biology, and in particular Evolution, indicates that the Principle operating in the sustenance of human life is no different from that sustaining all Life. When we let our consciousness dwell on this we may attain realization of the Unity of all Life and see that our belief in the separate existence of the 'me' and hence all dualistic thinking is based on a fundamental delusion.

Until comparatively recently the main stream of life had

always been unconscious of itself. The discursive intellect developed only relatively late in the evolution of life. The cerebral powers of man emerged through the activity of the Principle which ever strives at improved adaptation of the organism to the environment. Primarily, therefore, the intellect served the purpose of directly or indirectly sustaining mans vegetative existence in providing him with the capacity to secure food, shelter and clothing in the face of more or less antagonistic forces.

But, what do we see has happened? Man has on the whole succeeded so magnificently in safeguarding his material needs that amongst large numbers of civilized people the individual's conscious activities are no longer centred around the struggle for physical survival. The excess of cerebral energy which has become available is now diverted into other channels—channels which are no longer based on the original evolutionary pattern, on Reality. Man now lives firmly in the illusory belief of his own separate identity and most of his mental energies go towards purely egotistical self-affirmation. All his unhappiness, all his problems occur in this unreal world of his own making. Krishnamurti said much the same thing when he stated: 'Beyond the physical needs, any form of desire—for greatness, for truth, for virtue —becomes a psychological process by which the mind builds the idea of the "me" and strengthens itself at the centre.'*

We see then that, originally intended to fortify his existence, the discursive intellect of man is now the sole source of his unhappiness and has even become an undermining influence to his physical existence, witness the many who are suffering from psychosomatic disturbances of one kind or another. This development may well be another example of what Evolution has already taught us: where a form of life grows too specialized, it loses its virility and the fitness to maintain itself; eventually it perishes through its own over-specialization.**

This then appears to be the general evolutionary trend of

* *The First and Last Freedom*, p. 103.
** This process of decay is not only noticeable phylogenetically, but also ontogenetically, i.e. in the life history of the individual; and particularly so in those cases where the analytical mind dominates at the exclusion of everything else—as so often happens in the case of the scientist, the specialist, the intellectual, whose understanding is merely

the human species. In the following chapter we shall consider in how far this represents the whole picture and whether there is perhaps not a brighter side to it, the coming into being of a new factor that may counteract this general deterioration process of the mind.

academic. Sometimes the individual concerned becomes aware himself of a change in the latter part of his life, and a good example of this is afforded by a private communication written towards the end of his life by Charles Darwin, the famous biologist. He complains in it about a 'curious and lamentable loss of the higher aesthetic tastes', and states: 'My mind seems to have become a kind of machine for grinding general laws out of large collections of facts, but why this should have caused the atrophy of that part of the brain alone, on which the higher tastes depend, I cannot conceive.' It is interesting to note that Darwin himself seems to suspect that the observed deterioration has something to do with the excessive use of the analytical mind, but, ironically, the father of the theory of evolution has failed to understand how this biological evolution affects man psychologically.

21

ZEN AND SCIENCE

As we have seen, in Zen we have gone beyond knowledge, beyond thought, and one may properly state that when thought is thus transcended there emerges a valuable thing which we can only denote as 'no-knowledge' or Prajna. Now it is my contention that the *trend of organized knowledge leads, almost imperceptibly, towards a Zen outlook.*

If we look at the development of thinking as it has proceeded in the West from Copernicus to Einstein, we see that the role of the human observer is ever becoming less important philosophically; it has finally become very attenuated in the twentieth century. It could also be said that our world has become ever less anthropocentric—if I may be allowed to coin this useful expression.

In modern physics, for example, in finding out about the electron and other elementary particles our observations, as I have already pointed out, can only provide us with valid information up to a certain point. Beyond that, if we want to obtain an even more accurate and final determination of say, the position of an electron in space and time, the actual endeavour of procuring this further information has the effect of completely blurring the data obtained. In other words: a double-bind position has come about: the more we try to pin down the electron, the more it eludes us. Is not this a typical Zen situation, where we also find that the more we try to have Zen, the more our very trying prevents us from getting it.

I cannot resist the temptation in this connection to mention briefly two more examples of situations in modern physics which are veritable koans in the way they confound the intellect. Both refer to light and they are the following.

According to experimental results—and without going

into details—light behaves both as corpuscles and as waves. This means that sometimes it behaves as though it consisted of corpuscles, at other times as though it consisted of waves —this according to the type of experiment which is performed. Modern physicists accept this dual nature of light (they talk about 'wavicles') and no longer try to form a visualized concept of it. What in fact has happened is that without being aware of it they have acted in the spirit of Zen and transcended all concepts of the matter.

A second example is the very Zennish situation which Einstein brought home to us with regard to the constancy of the speed of light. The koan here could be formulated as follows: How is it that however fast I travel towards a particular light source, light proceeding from it at 186,000 miles per second will never reach my eye with a greater velocity than this; receding from the light source, light will never reach my eye with a lesser velocity? The whole of the relativity theory is based upon the forementioned absurdity, and relates physical events by means of a four-dimensional system of geometry. The equations fit, of course, but nobody can visualize what they represent.

This then is today the situation in science which is basically nothing but systematized common-sense—leading us to conclusions which to all appearances are insoluble by the intellect, in other words: complete nonsense. The question now arises: why is modern science, like Zen, a paradox? Why is it no longer straightforward common sense? Why can a spade no longer be called a simple spade—and yet we feel it will always be only just that.

The paradox, it seems to me, has arisen—as in Zen— because at last the limits of discursive thinking and hence the expression of Reality by means of 'concepts' has been reached. It appears then that the old physical laws and concepts were adequate enough only so long as they served as approximations. But when we approach the limits of our space-time world—the infinitely small and the infinitely large (the velocity of light is according to Einstein the largest possible velocity in the Universe)—these laws and concepts all break down, and we are left with a series of paradoxes. As in Zen, the final truth is not to be grasped for the reason that that which wants to grasp it is also part of that which is to be grasped.

It would, I think, be rather appropriate to conclude this essay with a quotation from Maurice Percheron in his book *Buddha and Buddhism*, which appears to contain some of the same insights which we have obtained in the course of our present investigation. 'Modern science, in its physico-chemical branch, has recently supported Buddhism,' he writes (p. 167).

'Not only has the image of the universe which our senses offer us been replaced by another image through knowledge of atomic physics, but also, on a philosophical plane, an insoluble dilemma arises from this new conception of the world. The energy data can only be established, in fact, by mathematical formulæ, that is, by a mental process that speaks of nth dimensions which are inconceivable although they square with the equations. Now the human mind intervenes in these theoretical constructions; and so the problem arises of whether the mathematical physics conceived by the mind is true, as we find ourselves, as in Buddhism, faced with the impossibility of deeming our conception of an object valid if the subject is confused with it. Bertrand Russell has illustrated this by showing the incapacity of the brain to examine its own functioning.

'This calling in question of knowledge is no less than the scientific recognition of Maya, i.e. of the relativity of realities. To get beyond the barrier erected by the subject-object confusion, our only hope of escape is on a transcendental plane, detached from causality and the relation of the subject to the object studied.'

'And so we see physics joining Buddhism in its theory of universal flux, of the lack of substance inherent in matter, of impermanence, of fundamental error attaching to the testimony of the senses, and consequently of doubt over the validity of the mind's speculations. We also see modern psychology concerned only with an essentially labile psyche: a fluid personality governed by temporary conjunctions escaping all control, and depending more or less on circumstances, acts and thoughts either barely acknowledged or not acknowledged at all.'

The only comment I would like to make on this quotation from Percheron is about his statement that science supports Buddhism. This is, of course, a logical necessity just as the reverse would be which is also true: 'Buddhism supports science', for Buddhism—like science—came about by being based entirely on the facts of experience, and it would therefore be impossible for the one to contradict the other. Thus it seems more to the point to say that Buddhism and science both have much in common although the former goes further and can be seen as the transcending of the latter. However, there is one sense in which science can be said to support Buddhism particularly: When science becomes introspective in an integral manner, instead of merely analytical, it can demonstrate by logical means where its own limitations lie in any particular direction, and by the mere fact of doing so it will already have caused its adept to set the first step on the road towards transcending these limitations, and thus have sparked off the beginning of a Zen consciousness, an understanding on a level even more fundamental than that of science.

Finally, it seems reasonable therefore to expect that Zen will find ever more fertile soil for healthy growth in this modern scientific age; and that it may thus be destined to exert a powerful counter-influence to the general deterioration in the quality of living which is the result of man's over-intellectualization.

ADDENDUM

Perhaps it may help the reader to attempt to summarize here what has been said in the last five chapters.

(1) The concepts of common sense and non-sense have been examined in relation to each other and to Zen Buddhism; the emergence of the paradox in the ultimate meaning of both science and Zen has been pointed out.

(2) An approach to epistemology has been developed which is based on the facts of experience. It is first shown that the subject as a functionally and spatially separate entity does not exist; the same is then shown to be true for the object. It is concluded that any form of dualism, whether that of body/mind or subject/object antitheses, is based on certain unwritten assumptions, which on closer examination appear to be arbitrary and un-

warranted. A parallel development in science is indicated, leading to what has been designated by the new concept 'space-time
barrier'.

(3) The present human situation has been considered from both
a psychological and a general biological point of view. It is
shown that modern science tends towards a Zen outlook, both
through historical necessity and by virtue of its findings in the
field of sub-atomic physics.

22

JUST THINKING

It has been said that the most exciting pastime of all is thinking. I would suggest there is one even more exciting: thinking about thinking, and not only exciting but what is more, liberating, because it is the only thing that can free us from the domination of thought—or rather, of second thought. If we do this we are treading the Way of Zen, whether we have heard the word 'Zen' or not.

Now why and how do our thoughts dominate us? Our thoughts come and go; yet, all our moods and feelings—and to a certain extent even our bodily functions—are the results of what, we think, is the 'impact' of these thoughts on ourselves. As long as we believe that, we have established a relationship: *me* and my *thoughts*, and as long as there is only relationship and no integration there can be no absolute freedom; on the contrary, there is ever present fear and psychological insecurity. Under these circumstances all we can do is to start working on our thoughts, by disciplining, repressing, fighting, trying to escape from them, etc. Yet all these efforts do not lead to freedom, to peace of mind—as we can all find out for ourselves; in fact, we see that they do just the opposite: they create more conflict, more struggle and more delusion.

However obvious it is that this dualistic approach cannot lead anywhere, yet, from the earliest moment in our lives that we started thinking, we have been thinking on dualistic lines: me and my thoughts; me and the objects of the outside world. Even the greatest thinkers have fallen into this trap. When Descartes postulated 'I think, therefore I am' he went further than was justified. All he was entitled to postulate was: 'I think, therefore thought or consciousness exists'. 'Something' exists all right, but is it 'I'—the 'I' as a separate entity

distinct from anything else existent? Yet, you see, Descartes'
jumping to conclusions is terribly instructive because it
teaches us so clearly that dualism is inherent in speech and
thought. The very process of thought is cutting up, dividing,
classifying and naming; in other words it *is* dualism.

Now, is there another way? As said in the beginning—
when we begin to think about thinking, that is where there
lies hope. Because if we fully understand thought, the false
processes of liberation will come to an end. We shall then
see that we are all that we know, in short—psychologically,
we *are* our thoughts: the thinker and the thought are one. We
shall then clearly see that most of the thoughts we have are
not worth thinking, because they themselves ensue directly
from the wrong concept which the empirical self holds
about itself. (The reason that it is so hard to get out of this is
obviously because we are caught in something that amounts
to nothing less than a vicious circle; communication
engineers talk in this connection so tellingly about 'closed-
circuit thinking'.) The thoughts I am referring to are all those
second thoughts—part of a continuous internal emotive and
imaginative film—resulting from the efforts of the empirical
self to strengthen itself, to give itself the appearance of con-
crete, enduring reality, by building up psychological memory
with experiences and beliefs—a process which very
efficiently precludes us from looking at things as they are,
from experiencing reality in the here and now. When we
really see all this and completely understand, we shall have
attained the end of psychological suffering, we shall have
Zen, we shall be absolutely and not merely conditionally
free.

23

THE POWER OF THOUGHT

Now, why are we possessed by our thoughts? We all know that thoughts come and go, that one thought will be replaced by another as inevitably as night follows day; for that reason alone there is no point in giving one thought more importance than another, since all thoughts are equally transient in the same manner that the objects of our thoughts are transient.

Yet, most of us are inclined to assign more importance to certain of our thoughts than to others, with the result that these same thoughts will recur again and again in different forms, so that finally we are 'carried away' by our own thoughts. In fact the difference between the ordinary man and the man who has Zen may be described almost completely by stating that the latter is never carried away, is never obsessed, by his thoughts: for he is ever mindful.

We have to ask ourselves, then, what kind of thoughts it is that assume this undue importance in our minds, so that they dominate and enslave us. If we can understand that, then perhaps we can break their hold and become free once again as we were at one time in our childhood: before thought began to exercise its tyranny over us. It appears that the type of thought which is concerned here is always of the kind that is part of a process of becoming in our minds. In other words these are thoughts that bear some direct relationship to the centre of the 'me'—it is as though this centre stands or falls by their outcome.* They are usually the typical second thoughts that sneak in and remain largely on a lower level of consciousness—if not entirely in the subconscious— and so are not sufficiently dealt with in the here and now.

---

* Hubert Benoit in his work *The Supreme Doctrine*, London, Routledge, 1955, talks about an 'inner lawsuit' which is continually being enacted in our subconscious mind.

This results in their leaving a considerable psychological residue which in turn will give rise to further second thoughts, and so on *ad infinitum*.

So we see that at the root of it all lies the restless activity of the self to become something which it is not, to hold on to what it thinks it has 'got' and to expand itself in order to further its chances in the so-called 'struggle for survival'. It has thus become apparent what harm can be done when something which is no more than an empirical entity, which has functional usefulness on the physical plane, begins to consider itself as though it were an absolute entity, and thus claims for itself existence as a psychological 'entity', which means that it gets caught in the inevitable vicious circle of ambition, urge for security and fear. Then life is lived in delusion and this process—once set in—is very difficult to break.

Now if we have understood the problem it must be obvious that there is only a problem because of the false premise that there is a self to be protected, an entity separate from our thoughts. Once the falseness of this proposition is seen there is no longer any problem; it means freedom from the restless activity of the mind—the ending of the fruitless self-enclosing process and the beginning of that which lies beyond time and beyond separateness or duality. Then detachment, which some of us have tried vainly to cultivate for many years, will have become a fact of its own accord.

24

CAN WE SEEK, CAN WE CONTROL HAPPINESS?

Most of us think we can find happiness, peace of mind, by ensuring an unbroken series of gratifications for the ever-changing desires in our lives. And we do not realize it is exactly this outlook which is responsible for 'dukkha', psychological suffering; that it is this *seeking* for happiness which causes the unhappiness.

Now let us look into this matter of desires more closely. Suppose we have a desire to achieve object A and we think this is necessary, essential for our happiness. In other words, we, the controllers, can by the action which springs from our desire, control the world outside us to achieve a certain result which, we think, will give us some happiness.

We are so used to this process of the controller and the controlled on the physiological level; for example, we feel hungry, so we take food and feel satisfied—we feel cold and uncomfortable, so we switch on the heater and feel warm and comfortable, etc. Now we think we can apply the same method to our psychological being. We feel unhappy—so through certain control of the environment we can feel happy. But is this analogy real or false? That is the problem we have to find out.

First of all, are there, in the psychological sphere two distinctly separate entities, the controller and the controlled; otherwise it will not be possible for the action of control to take place. Although I state: 'I have a desire for object A', there is no entity apart from the desire; in other words I *am* this desire for object A. There is no question of 'me' controlling this desire because there is only one process; me and my desire are one and consequently one cannot control the other. I may possibly do something which will lead to my achieving object *A* and thus to the so-called satisfaction of my desire for object *A*—which will simply mean that the desire will no longer be there—only to be replaced by desire for object *B*, and so on *ad infinitum*.

Whereas in the physical and material sphere, I (that is to say, my body) can enrich myself by action, by control of the outside world, in the psychological sphere I cannot enrich myself; all that happens is a sequence of psychological states whereby it is meaningless to speak of enrichment or gathering happiness for oneself. A failure to see that our desires are part of a series of rapidly following psychological states will produce frustration and unhappiness, and will strengthen the delusion of a separate 'me' independent of our thoughts and experiences. In actual fact this whole false analogy has come about exactly through the verbal confusion which arises when we say *I* or *my* mind: we think we are referring to definite separate entities similar to 'my body', 'my hand'; in short we have made the false premise that there is a separate 'me'.

It is therefore essential to appreciate this fundamental difference in our control of physical and psychological factors. In the physical world, my body and the outside object I want to control may be considered for practical purposes as two different physical 'entities' but in the psychological sphere 'I' and my desire or my desire satisfied are not different but identical. Therefore there is not a controller and that which is controlled; to try to effect control in the psychological sphere is therefore like a dog trying to catch its own tail—resulting in it going round and round in circles.

Complete realization of the above, not only intellectually, but on all levels so that we feel it as it were in our bones, will cause a transformation to take place: the mind will see the futility of all striving for happiness and this will result in a let-go, a weakening all round of all psychological desires which in turn will lead to the dissolving of the false 'me'. This will mean the beginning of wisdom and the possibility of bliss.

ON LIBERATION

When using the word 'liberation' we must realize once again the restrictions imposed by verbalization. The term is in a way quite misleading since it does not at all express the actual experience. Experiencing liberation is experiencing what we have always been, our natural, happy state of being. The word in question is a very good illustration of the relativity of all terminology. The actual experience has now the appearance of liberation since after a lifetime of conditioning and hypnotizing ourselves with wrong thinking, our artificial, deluded, unhappy state of being does not seem to us an acquired state but now 'feels' as our natural state, from which—being unhappy and frustrated—we naturally want to be liberated; whereas in real fact this 'liberation' was never necessary if only we let go of our acquisitions, of that which is false in our outlook. And after all, if there never was a self how can there be liberation from the self?

Is it not instructive in this context to observe the obvious manifestations of 'joie de vivre', or joy of living, so typical of youth—not, I suggest, because of lack of responsibilities, but because there we are observing a natural, spontaneous state of functioning, not yet corrupted and twisted by habits of wrong thinking which have all led the centre of the 'me' to acquire an importance which it should never have had.

DESIRES

Our desires perpetuate themselves like a chain reaction—as long as they are not understood for what they are: the blustering efforts of the self to assert itself, to find some security and some permanency in an impermanent world. And not only do we tolerate domination by our desires but worse still: we are attached to them—since we feel that as long as we fill our lives with sensations, experiences, or rather the memories of these, we escape from feeling the emptiness, the nothingness of our essential being. For we sense in some dim sort of a way the real nature of our being but consciously 'interpret' it according to our 'outlook on life'—which is the result of life-long conditioning, of being under the sway of powerful psychological memories, in short of previous manifestations of the self.

The whole point of Zen is to break this vicious circle, and to look at things as they really are—recognizing the emptiness and nothingness of what we are, seeing into the essential nature of the 'self'. Although it appears simple when studied academically, to carry this out in practical living is extremely difficult, because it entails the breaking of attitudes, habits and reflexes acquired during a lifetime.

LIVING BY ZEN

'If one knows but does not act accordingly, one
knows imperfectly.'

The difficulty in following the Zen way is that it is a path
which is not of time and therefore not a 'way' in the ordinary
sense of the word. Hence our ordinary devices and gimmicks
to 'get by' are of no avail here. Knowledge, being the known,
and therefore of the past, cannot help us, but only understanding can. But the difficulty is that even when complete
understanding has been achieved this is only of momentary
value and as soon as the self asserts itself again, the process
of complete understanding has to be experienced afresh in
order to liberate the moment—and in that process memory
cannot assist but in fact will only hinder us.

When in this manner the self has been squashed repeatedly
it will understand its own futility and essential unreality so
completely (both on the conscious and subconscious levels)
that a transformation will take place spontaneously. This
transformation is not the destruction or the repression of the
self but is its transcendence: an awakening as to its true
identity, and hence the freedom from its demands and
accumulations. Only then will it be possible to live from
moment to moment and be free from the bondage of time.

A SCIENTIST LOOKS AT BUDDHISM

(BUT ALSO: A BUDDHIST LOOKS AT SCIENCE)

A scientist who looks at Buddhism must at once notice some striking similarities that exist between science and Buddhism. In the first place both are silent regarding the question whether there is God or not; there is neither affirmation nor denial on this point. It is perhaps correct to say that it is not so much that they are totally unconcerned with this matter, as the realization that the problem cannot be put in such simple terms without becoming quite meaningless: to the really important questions in life there can be no simple answer 'yes' or 'no', and moreover, very often the question is 'not a legitimate one in the first place.

Then again both are firmly based on experience. There is a statement by Dr D. T. Suzuki to the effect that there is nothing in Buddhism which is not based on experience. Both science (with the exception of mathematics) and Buddhism are practical and deal with the world as it actually is (or was), and not with some hypothetical, ideal world. Both shun speculation about the future, but on the other hand they confidently make predictions which are firmly based on the laws of cause and effect.

I said with the exception of mathematics—but then mathematics should be considered to be only a useful tool, an auxiliary, not a basic, science—a means to an end. Mathematics, as is well known, deals with an 'ideal' world built up from such elements as a dimensionless point, a line of one dimension, the square root of minus one, etc. These are imaginary concepts arrived at through extrapolation (i.e.

'idealization') of basic realities observed in the physical world.

So far we have dealt only with the similarities between science and Buddhism; let us now probe a little deeper and see where they differ. In Buddhism we are concerned with the destruction of ignorance, delusion, in order to uncover, Truth, Reality. Now many people would say that this is also the concern of science, that science is the pursuit of Truth. So let us examine this viewpoint for if we are at all serious, we must leave no stone unturned in our search for the Unknown, and if science provides us with a valid approach then we should be able to make use of it.

Firstly, what do we mean by Truth, Reality? The question will have to be considered whether we can define 'Reality'. If we try, we shall soon find this is impossible, for we would have to define Reality, as manifested by the phenomenal world, in terms of phenomena. However, like can never be adequately defined by like but only by something more fundamental than itself; our efforts will seem like catching the wind in our fist! Furthermore, since any conception of Reality we can have is necessarily based on evidence supplied by the sense organs, we may be asked such awkward questions as: 'How can you be sure that your sense organs do not deceive you?' 'What is the evidence worth, anyway?', and worse still: 'Is a dream real?'—questions which nobody can answer satisfactorily.

Now, as we have seen in earlier chapters, any statement I make about the nature of the universe is necessarily based on relativities; therefore, absolutely speaking, it is not true. For although the mind likes to believe it has a fixed point somewhere, a first absolute truth upon which it can base all its reasoning, in actual fact there is none (cf., the conclusion of the Prajnaparamita: 'All things should be regarded as in a dream'). Therefore Reality will always be incapable of definition.

On the basis of this conclusion I can now postulate, for the sake of convenience, that there are different levels of reality (all based upon relativities), and an Absolute Reality, which transcends them all, but which is not knowable by the mind. Within the framework of conceptualized thought, the postulation of such an absolute Reality, the Unknown, is logically justified, for as soon as we talk about 'relativities' there is the underlying idea of an Absolute in which these relativities exist. Whether there is, in fact, such an absolute Reality apart from being a concept in the mind, that is a different matter—and, after all, only verifiable by personal experience.

However, the postulate that there are different levels of reality will prove a very useful one. For example, we feel that a dream is not 'true', yet it is a very real thing. It can now be stated that the dream is not on the same level of reality as a fact of my waking experience; yet that 'fact' can be as unsubstantial as a dream in comparison with the Absolute. Similarly can I deal with a lie, with any fabrication of the imagination. The self, i.e. the idea I carry with me about myself, is not true, yet it is a very real thing to me—so real that all the self-limiting activities of my mind are based upon it.

This last example is an important point to grasp, and because it is, as it were, the fundamental delusion from which all other delusions arise, it may be justified to elaborate this a little further. Because in everything we do and think we make the 'I' a fixed point, which it is not, we see everything wrongly. For example, we all strive so hard to be successful in the world; yet, do we ever ask ourselves the simple question: Why should I be 'successful', which really means 'exclusive' (cf. the term 'outstanding' as virtually synonymous with 'successful'), and why should I not be ordinary? But we never stop to consider upon what foundations our activities are based. On the contrary, too often we are even prepared to kill one another—and even ourselves, via stomach ulcers and stress diseases—for this elusive prize of success, or perhaps merely to keep up with the Joneses.

And when there are disturbances in our life, all we do is to escape by throwing ourselves into some form of distraction, instead of asking ourselves the question: Why should I *not* be disturbed? Finally, do we ever enquire into the meaning of such ideas as 'having success' and 'suffering'? And if we really want to go to the bottom of these things, we shall have to face the question: What is it that has success? What is it that suffers? Then we shall find that both 'suffering' and 'having success' are merely forms of agitation, the movements of the self—an entity that is no more real than a dream.

Thus we see that because we have never recognized different levels of reality, the relativities have been taken for the real, and so the mind is constantly gripped by illusion in its many manifestations. Our condition is that we go from one illusion to another, without ever realizing that each time our point of departure, upon which our seeking is based, is false. Hence any new conclusion we arrive at is also false—and so we go on in our restlessless.

What makes it even more tragic is that we are actually half aware of this process, but we *like* to be held by illusion —for we think it lends colour to our lives. We think that without it, life would be so stale, so suffocating, and that this is the best we can do with our life, anyway. In this connection it may be instructive to relate a discussion I once had about Buddhism with a person of considerable intellectual attainment. He conceded that Buddhism was true, for it was based on the inescapable facts of life, but he added: 'I don't like existing like a vegetable.' But how did he know what this would be like, if he had never tasted this state? Perhaps the vegetative existence 'has' something which we do not know, and without which we are all the poorer. How do we know what it is like to live in Reality instead of in Illusion, if we have never had the experience, not even for a short moment?

Our enquiry so far has led us to discover that the mind can only know uncertainty, empirical truth, and that therefore 'knowledge' cannot lead man to the Real. And after all, what *do* we know? Many people feel this lack of fundamental knowledge intuitively, but still think it is somehow restricted to certain fields. They may say, for instance: 'we don't even know what electricity is, we only know its effects.' But do we know anything but for its effects? Since all our knowledge is *about*, we always know things by their effects, and by their effects only.

At this stage we should be able to answer the question put earlier in this chapter, whether perhaps science can provide us with a valid approach to the Unknown. It must now be obvious, after all that has been said about knowledge, that science, too, can only give information about the world *on the relative plane*. The edifice of science is being erected brick by brick from relative truths, and however great, however dazzling and intellectually satisfying, will always remain relative, a product of the mind that classifies and correlates sense impressions, bound within the limits of space and time.*

I think it may be instructive in this connection to relate a controversy which recently took place in the correspondence columns of *The New Scientist*.** It started with a letter writer asking readers of this journal whether science should be considered the pursuit of truth, or whether it was perhaps something entirely different. Supposing an imaginary experiment were performed of weighing a glass vessel on a laboratory scale as accurately as possible, and then repeating the experiment on ever finer balances, would there come a time that the value thus obtained for the weight of the vessel would no longer change, because it would be the 'right' weight? In other words, his question was, is there such a thing as the absolutely correct weight, or is this merely a concept in our mind?

The answer is, of course, that we ourselves have created the concept of 'weight', quite arbitrarily on the basis of relativities, and that we cannot therefore expect an 'absolute' answer. There is in fact only a complex interrelation between the object, the mechanism of the balance, the force of gravity, the physical conditions pertaining at the time, and finally, our mind that wants to express this relationship quantitatively.

One of the persons who replied put his finger right on it when he wrote the following assessment of the 'scientific method':—

'To speak of a scientist as a seeker of truth is a colloquialism which, if interpreted too literally, may mislead us as to the correct nature of the physical world. The scientist, in attempting to explain a natural phenomenon, does not look for some underlying true phenomenon but tries to

---

* 'Scientific knowledge, so called, is not at all exhaustive and for that reason awaits further corrections, for it is confined to a sphere of its own limitations.'—Dr D. T. Suzuki in *Zen and Japanese Buddhism*, Tokyo, Japan Travel Bureau, 1958, p. 64.
** *The New Scientist*, January 28, 1960, p. 225.

invent a hypothesis or model whose behaviour will be as close as possible to that of the observed natural phenomenon. As his techniques of observation improve, and he realizes that the natural phenomenon is more complex than he originally thought he has to discard his first hypothesis, and replace it with another, more sophisticated one, which may be said to be 'truer' than the first, since it resembles the observed facts more closely.' (Compare this also with p. 47 of the present work.) Another writer stated that science must be seen as organized common sense rather than the pursuit of truth (and that the two need not necessarily be in agreement with each other the present writer has tried to show elsewhere in this work.)

It must be clear, therefore, that the scientist is simply seeking a new hypothesis which fits the observed phenomena better than did a previous one; but this is still within the sphere of 'models' of the universe, of reality—and that is all he is concerned with. Therefore, he is *not* seeking Truth, for if he were he would at once give up the effort to 'reconstruct' reality by means of models and mathematical equations which at best can only have the same relation to Reality as a photographic image has to its original (it lacks a full dimension!). In other words the scientist lives in a world of abstractions; he is only concerned with 'making things work' by systematized common sense. Basically he is a 'concept merchant' for the concepts give him the results he is seeking.*

Whereas the seeker for Truth cannot have a motive or be seeking a result—for if that were his attitude he would be held by both motive and anticipation of result, and so no longer be free to discover—the scientist (contrary to popular opinion) is utilitarian. He has a motive, namely, a practical application—or in the case of 'fundamental research', he wants to satisfy an equation or a hypothesis (which is always a pre-conceived scientific notion or 'idea'), or, generally speaking, fill out existing knowledge. All this may perhaps be somewhat crudely put, but it is a fact that science cannot operate in a mental vacuum, in emptiness. Science

* The following statement by Dr Suzuki seems relevant: 'Science means systematization, and Zen is just its reverse. Words are needed in science and philosophy, but they are a hindrance in Zen. Why? Because words are representations and not realities, and realities are what is most highly valued in Zen.' op. cit., p. 64.

needs ideation, it is based upon the process of conceptualized thought, in fact it *is* that process.

Buddhism—or perhaps one should say, the spiritual life—on the other hand, can only operate in this essential vacuum, the creative emptiness which comes about when the mind, the discursive intellect, has been slain. For Truth is not something that can be apprehended within the narrow confines of the subject-object duality; it is not something that can be measured, thought or communicated. Therefore, the way of knowledge, of science, will never touch it.

We can now conclude our enquiry by stating that for all their similarity science and Buddhism are operating in different dimensions; there can therefore never be any conflict between them. The method of science, as we have seen, is not the 'method' of Buddhism, but perhaps it is valid to state that the 'spirit' of scientific investigation, i.e. the application of the scientific method without being emotionally involved, without attachment to it, is identical with the 'spirit of enquiry' in Zen. Furthermore, the scientist has already learned not to be deceived by the surface appearance of things but to look for a deeper, hidden level of reality in them. When the latter process is driven to its logical conclusion, he will eventually be looking for that 'level' which transcends all levels. Thus, as we have already shown in another chapter of this work, the trend of scientific thinking tends inevitably towards the Zen realization.

Hence a certain 'affinity of mind' can sometimes be noted between scientists and Zen Buddhists, but this has nothing to do with intellectual capability, it is more a matter of 'character', of attitude towards life. It is in that sense only, that one could say that the scientist is in spirit a seeker of truth, for he 'uses' the concepts without being bound by them; he seeks a result but is not emotionally tied up with it; he is an observer of natural phenomena who completely refrains from value 'judgments', in other words, he has transcended 'good' and 'bad' where it concerns his data. At least potentially, many of our scientists are Zen Buddhists in spirit, without knowing it!

Where science is the pursuit of knowledge *about* the world (therefore, within the framework of space and time), Buddhism is concerned with 'knowing', with the Absolute and it has no need of going through the Relative first in order to contact the Absolute: it begins where science ends —with the breaking down of the subject-object duality. Science can give us material and intellectual benefits, various kinds of comforts, but not Reality. And it is only when man has made contact with the Absolute and lives in Reality, that there can be a happiness which is not merely the opposite of suffering, a bliss which transcends all opposites and is therefore independent of the phenomenal world—because it is the release from the painful cramp of ordinary 'I'-consciousness.

29

THE SLAYING OF THE MIND

If, as we have seen in the previous chapter, the way of knowledge will never lead to enlightenment, what is one to do? If
to 'know' and to 'believe' (which after all are of the same
order, only we assign less 'certainty' to belief than to knowledge, but even the most certain knowledge implies a
modicum of belief) are foredoomed as effective 'ways', and
if in fact any act of mentation is a hindrance, should we perhaps 'slay the mind', kill it off by repressing or 'controlling'
every thought that enters it, so that in the end there is
nothing but emptiness, the Void?

The attempt to escape from our predicament by sheer
force of will-power, by control and discipline (so-called
'mind training') is understandable enough, for it is the same
process by which man succeeds in controlling and moulding
his environment to his ends. Hence it is thought that this
might also be an effective means to subdue the mind. But is
the analogy valid?

It seems to me that the disciplining of the mind as a way to
liberation is not essentially different from the ways of
knowledge and belief, for this again is based upon dualistic
thought, the mistaken notion that there is a permanent entity
in us that stands aloof, and can repress and control the
thoughts occurring if it wishes to do so.

This is such an important point and the basis of so many
false ways of liberation, that it is worth while to look into it
a little more closely. When we worry, is there a separate
entity that observes 'worries' and is bothered by them; or is
the mind totally composed of worries, and is the observing
entity just an illusion, a trick of the mind? When we experience, are we ever aware of an 'experiencer' independent
of experience? Observing the process of our thoughts with

full attention, we shall see that there never is such a separate entity. This erroneous idea has come about because the idea I carry of myself continuously intervenes in between my experiences. (This remembering of the static 'I'-picture is of course another experience, a remembering without rememberer). Due to the incredible speed of thought both kinds of experiences get mixed up and associated (i.e. they start giving rise to each other) and this brings about the feeling of an 'I' that apparently can manipulate thought.

Thus the idea has arisen that I can become 'good' by repressing or controlling 'bad' thoughts;* and this is what priests of many denominations have tried to achieve for centuries, to mould the mind into a pre-conceived, ideal pattern of their own making. But since this kind of 'good' and 'bad' is based upon human reasoning, and therefore conditioned, the 'transformed' person will still be conditioned; there is only 'deformation' and no 'transformation'. In actual fact, 'disciplined' or 'undisciplined', our minds always live in a pattern (that of the individual's particular adaptation to the moulding, conforming force of Society). But from the point of view of Eternity, living in a pattern, of whatever kind, is ever detrimental, because Reality knows no pattern—it is fluid and unbounded. Since our minds are static—being made of the stuff of Time and therefore anchored in the past—and have therefore already something of death in them, there is ever a conflict between the two states: this causes the pain of living.

If it is fully realized that any of the conventional ways cannot lead us to the goal, we may be forced to accept a situation in which there is no system, no method of liberation—and start looking at the problem with fresh minds, i.e. without pre-conceived notions about our search.

First of all, what is it that we are seeking? For if we do not know what we are after, we shall be beaten before we have ever started the enquiry. Is it truth, however bitter, however discomforting, that we are after—or is it relief from

---

* Many people talk glibly about replacing 'bad' thoughts by 'good' thoughts without stopping to consider whether such a thing is possible at all. They are only concerned with the surface layer of the mind and they do not realize that every time they repress thought they 'shoot' it straight down into the subconscious to store up more trouble for later.

the sorrows of the world, some kind of satisfaction which will give us temporary oblivion to the pain of living? This is a most fundamental point to be clear about. If it is the latter we are seeking, if we are looking for a mental haven, we shall certainly find something, but it will not be Truth. What we shall find will have come forth from the mind, a projection of our own limited thinking, that can therefore never be the Real.

Unfortunately, most people in this world are only seeking a way out of their troubles, a relief from the pressures of daily living, and they will seize at anything that acts as an anodyne, that gives them some comfort; this anodyne may be in the form of a drug, some self-inflating activity that temporarily drowns their feeling of inadequacy, or perhaps a comforting belief (e.g. in a hereafter that will compensate them for this miserable existence on earth). All these are ways of escape and therefore afford only temporary relief—but deep down in the subconscious the conflict continues, for the deeper layers of the mind are not so easily deceived. Furthermore, every escape engenders its own subsequent reaction in the form of more pain, so there is a self-activating process at work.

The seeking of comfort and the seeking of truth are obviously incompatible; and since most people do the former, there are really very few amongst the so-called religious people who pursue the truth. For to pursue truth the first requirement is that we drop all the preconceived notions to which we are attached, that give us some feeling of security and 'respectability'—and that means 'living dangerously', something that few of us are prepared to do.

If, on the other hand, we are not merely seeking a haven, an escape—and there are much easier, more effective and less harmful ways of escape than through religion—if we are interested to find out without ulterior motives, then, I think, we shall find something of real value. To start with, we should be in a state of complete not-knowing, and not in any way tied to an urge to obtain a result. At the same time there should be an all-consuming, burning interest in discovering what Life is all about, a desire to go to the root of things, not being satisfied with superficial explanations: an overpowering doubt that questions everything, even one's own existence.

We normally look to the enlightened man for an answer to our problems—a key that can once and for all unlock the door to happiness. But perhaps we should even doubt this: maybe no such answer can be given, for the reason that there is no key, no method or system. So let us first look into the fundamental question: is there a Way to Reality? Is there a path that can be followed, a method that can be applied, so that eventually we shall reach the Goal?

Are not all these ideas based upon the wrong concept of 'time', for a method or system that can be applied presupposes time in which the method is proceeding to its successful completion. For example, as we have seen when we discussed 'mind training', we think we can use discipline, which is force, violence, in the beginning, to obtain peace, serenity, in the end. But discipline in itself can never give rise to serenity (for discipline implies resistance) no matter how long we practise. Thus time has become the transforming factor upon which we depend. But is there actually such a thing as 'time' at all, existing independently of us, or is time merely a yardstick? I think time is a product of the mind, in the same way that the 'yardstick' is only a piece of wood, were it not for its quite arbitrary use for measuring lengths. Just as we have created length, breadth and height, the dimensions of space, so we have created time as a yardstick for measuring change *in relation to a static world*. But since transience is a property of all things,* time is implicit in the nature of things and becomes unreal when postulated as existing explicitly, i.e. apart from things.

So the transforming factor lies in myself and operates from moment to moment and not progressively. It is not something that I bring into my life from the outside, whether as the emulation of an ideal or the application of a formula, a system. This then means the cessation of all my seeking, all my activities, all my 'doing' to liberate myself which only gives rise to resistance and more restraint. If I want freedom in the end I must *begin* by being free, unrestrained, and not in a state of conflict: I must completely 'let-go' of

---

* Since 'thingness' is a reflection of the nature of the mind, time is also implicit in mind; the same follows, of course, for space.

myself. That this must be so, can also be seen quite simply when we realize that the striving for salvation, for purification of the mind, or whatever you like to call it, is still for the achievement of *my* salvation, *my* purification, *my* spiritual progress, etc., and therefore a self-ish striving. It is in no way different from any other process of becoming, of acquisitiveness, and will thus achieve the exact opposite of what is aimed at; instead of losing the ego we are strengthening the 'me' at its roots.

Now, in my experience, people get very worried when told that they can do nothing, especially in the West where so much emphasis is laid on action for its own sake, on what is called euphemistically 'private enterprise', and where even enlightenment is regarded as an 'achievement'. But non-doing does not mean that you don't care about anything any longer and go to sleep. The misunderstanding, as always, is caused by the inadequacy of words in expressing mental processes or states. For one could say that when the very limit of conceptualized thought is reached, the doing becomes non-doing and the non-doing becomes doing, just like our normal state of living becomes death and that which seems to us like death at the moment becomes the supreme form of living.

The very same people who shout 'Quietism!' when told to do nothing, do not realize that there never is a single moment that they do nothing, and that they would not even be capable of this 'quietism'. For if their minds could only do absolutely nothing for one short moment, their problems would be solved;* then they would 'know', i.e. transcend the apparent conflict of the pair of opposites, doing/non-doing. The point is that we are so busy all the time comparing, condemning, judging the phenomena we perceive (all with reference to the static 'I'-picture; this is the nursing of our psychological feed-back system) that we are not even aware of this busyness anymore.

The answer to our enquiry may now have come quite unexpectedly and in a way 'simply'; for it is this continuous background noise, this chatter of the mind of which we are no longer aware that prevents us from complete non-doing.

* Cf. Goethe: 'Wann Du stille wirst, ist Dir geholfen.'

It is this same chatter that is responsible for the dreams when we sleep and the vicious, discriminating thoughts in our waking state which stand in the way to realization. The only possible solution is, of course, not to ask how to eliminate the mind's background but *to listen to it*, so that in that passive state of listening the awareness can have its own action, without us doing anything about it.* Our conclusion, then, is that only negative thought or passive alertness, which requires great sensitivity, may lead us to the experience of the silent mind. Then, when the mind, which is the cumulative response of the known, of our conditioning, ceases its activity, there is a possibility for that which is unconditioned, and therefore timeless, to come into being.

Moreover, when we understand all this, not merely intellectually and therefore superficially, but through experiencing it from moment to moment, a spontaneous relaxation of all that unconscious activity will come about. There will then be a moment of Total Attention because there is no longer any interference with the thoughts that come and go. Since there is no longer a fixed point in the mind, thoughts will no longer be strengthened or restrained, they will thus no longer give rise to resistance (and it is this 'resistance' that maintains the unreal self) but will pass smoothly and not recur. They will weaken in intensity and there will be fewer of them, leading to occasional gaps, moments of silence. Eventually the 'slaying of the mind', not through violence, but through non-interference, will have become a fact.

It is interesting in this connection to see the analogy between exhausting the force of one's opponent in Judo, and exhausting the force of one's desire, aversion, etc., in mindfulness. When this psychic energy is given free rein for one moment and thus spends itself, there is the stopping of the time-binding activities of the ego. The psychic force, born of ignorance, is, as it were, deprived of its fulcrum, the 'fixed point' of the mind, and thus can no longer exert its momen-

* Krishnamurti has written:—'To do is to avoid what *is*, and the avoidance of what *is* is the grossest form of stupidity . . . The doing is not important, but the listening is.' (*Commentaries on Living*, London, Gollancz, 1956, p. 165.)

tum to 'move' us; it is rendered completely harmless (compare also Takuan's discussion of the 'stopping' of the mind, footnote on p. 38). In that single moment of true mindfulness there is the stepping of out of time, the breaking of psychological continuity by completely living in the present, and so the stopping of the reflex mechanism of the mind that ever nurtures the 'me'.

30

'THERE IS NOTHING IN IT . . .'

What then is the balance of some few years' intensive searching, the study of religion in general and Buddhism in particular? Does one feel enriched, fortified with precious esoteric knowledge, secure in a newly-found wisdom? Not at all and on the contrary—all such ideas of enrichment, accumulation of virtue, and 'art of living' seem laughable and have been swept away for good.

When recently meeting a friend who had also studied the subject for some years, we both found ourselves echoing the same sentiment: 'There is nothing in it . . .' This, surprisingly and unexpectedly, comes as the final answer to our quest; we had expected to go a long way, and so we have— but lo and behold, we are back where we started! And when we said there is 'nothing in it', we did not mean just religion, but Life. The supreme Reality is nothingness, i.e. as conceived by Man, for it is indefinable and indescribable. Because no philosophy, no thoughts can hold it, Reality is Nothingness to the thinking mind.

But almost in the same breath with the admission that the final answer had proved Empty, it was stated that our whole outlook had fundamentally changed, and life could never be the same again. As though there had been the opening of a third eye, the world was seen for the first time as it really is, unobscured by the screen of ideation which normally results from our 'purposive philosophy' of life, our efforts to 'get somewhere'. All experience had now acquired an unexpected richness of content, a vividness and intensity which is the direct result of completely living in the present moment—an experience unadulterated by anticipation of the future or brooding over the past.

This is the great paradox of Zen, and of Life. The very

negation which seems implied in Nothingness, the Void, signifies at once its absolute confirmation. Only when man stands completely alone, in absolute nakedness, and is left to face himself devoid of any attachments, any dependence on external supports, can there be a wholehearted 'yes' to Life. Until the emptiness of all attachments, of all efforts at building 'security' is realized, there can be no cessation of the feeling of insecurity. Until it is seen that any of our so-called 'successes' or victories are empty there can be no peace of mind and no enlightenment. Hence Krishnamurti states: 'To succeed is always to fail. Arrival is death and travelling is eternal. To gain, to be victorious in this world, is to lose life.' It is also in this context that the words of Christ be-come quite clear, when he speaks about the need for 'be-coming like nothing'. Only when we are 'nothing' in our-selves can there be complete harmony with a Reality which is 'nothingness', the cessation of all conflict and con-tradiction in the mind. It is because we are ambitious and all want to be 'something' that there is suffering and strife in the world; it is the logical outcome of wanting to place oneself outside Reality and to go against Nature. Because of its impossibility there is pain.

Religion turns out to be one large zero; yet this very dis-covery is of revolutionary significance. The implication is that what is important is the process of investigation, it is this which liberates—not the result of the investigation. Once we have passed through this phase even the concept of Buddhism or Zen as 'something' is piled on to the rubbish heap of wasteful ideation. Consider in this connection Krishnamurti's statement: 'To the seeker of Reality there is neither Christ nor Buddha, there is only himself and his effort to find Truth'; and Christ's admonition: 'Seek and ye shall find'. And how can we be free to discover if we are tethered to some formula, a belief, an assumption, or an ideal?

Zero and Infinity are mathematically related symbols. Zen, Life, when pressed for an answer, gives out only a zero, yet at the same time it is Infinity, for it is the Whole that is limitless. In practice this signifies that in the final negation of the clamour of the mind for a description, a definition, of the Unknown, we discover that everything has become pregnant with meaning. Then the invitation of the Master, 'have a cup of tea', becomes in its extreme purposelessness as full of meaning as, for example, the act of getting married and having children. It is only when it is fully realized that Life has no purpose, that Life just *is*, that our personal life acquires a meaning, a new 'fullness'—and *that* realization is the fulfilment of individual existence. Until this realization dawns upon us, life is just one long, dreary series of struggles, conflicts and sufferings—in short, a life not worth living.

When the world is no longer seen in terms of 'things' and 'ideas' (which state is called the 'slaying of the mind' in Zen), we can fully apprehend the retort of one famous Zen Master to another: 'After all, there isn't much in your Buddhism . . .' and the admonition of another Master: 'Every time you utter the name Buddha wash out your mouth.' And even to say that the ultimate truth of Buddhism is 'nothingness' is beside the point, for isn't this too, an idea? And Zen will have nothing of abstractions, or anything not directly based on experience. So we read of the monk who thought he understood Buddhism and stated that he could no longer lay his hands on 'anything' (he meant that the thingness of the world no longer existed for him) whereupon the Master answered 'Oh, yes?, Well *I* can lay my hands on something all right!', thereby pulling the nose of the poor monk as hard as he could. At that very moment the mind of the monk was jolted into realization.

When all is said and done, Zen is the concreteness of everyday life. So when a monk finds himself in a lonely hut with no fuel to burn to keep warm but a wooden statue of the Buddha, he burns this . . . for isn't the statue a piece of wood that admirably serves the purpose of the moment? 'Nothing is holy' Bodhidharma had thundered to the Emperor Wu, who was under the mistaken impression that 'devotion' and 'good works' constituted the highest forms of religious life. So why shouldn't the poor monk warm his frozen limbs in the way he did? In the same category is the charming little story about the monk who was so holy that even the birds made their offerings to him. One day this monk had an interview with his Master, which completely opened his eye to the truth; from that day onward nobody, not even the birds, made him any more offerings.

Enough has now been said about the subject to show that in the end there can only be Silence; when no longer anything is said or done to describe or 'act' Zen consciously, is there the experience of the silent mind, in which there is constant renewal so that the mind is ever fresh and innocent. So let us wash out our mouths many times, for we have mentioned the Buddha, Christ, etc., many times, and consider ourselves lucky that this time we shall be spared the pulling of the nose, the thirty blows or suchlike treatment— for who could deny that we have deserved it? Thus there remains only to 'walk on!'

SOME THOUGHTS ON LIFE

RECORDED DURING 1958/59

The spiritual life is a tender plant; it will not grow on a soil contaminated with self. Yet all our social values encourage and cultivate the self.

It seems to me that not only is the social world we live in one of delusion, but worse: it is a world of make-belief. The pretension *must* be kept up at any cost, for without this make-belief man cannot life; he would rather die than face reality. Hence the emotional, hostile reaction when man is confronted with the truth of life, which is the truth about himself.

Love *is* blind, because it is not of the mind; it is often confused with passion which *makes* blind.

What is called 'matter' is that part of Reality of which man becomes conscious through the senses (primarily through vision and touch). Matter in the traditional sense of the word, matter *per se* does not, of course, exist (nor does the so-called 'thing-in-itself'—that bogey of Emmanuel Kant —exist). Hence, the division of the world in material and non-material entities is meaningless and has to be revised. This fallacious division is a direct result of our prevalent dualistic world outlook.

Thought, by its very nature, must always be unreal, since it is nothing if it does not divide, cut up and separate that which is neither divisible nor indivisible, neither One nor the Many, that which cannot be translated into concepts. Hence, we can only 'describe' Reality in negative terms: 'neti, neti' (not this, not that . . .).

In considering whether being alive is Good, we must realize that what matters is not what the mind thinks about being, but only the experience of being. And this experience can only be had when the mind is not.

All psychological desire is a conditioned reflex.

Our imaginative life is only real in the sense that a lie is real. Desire, imagination, the mind, is never Reality—it is always either past or future, for it always operates through memory, through recognition.

There are two attitudes which must be considered luxuries (and hindrances). They are the academic study of religion, and the reading of books on Zen, etc., simply to take cognisance of certain terms and descriptions of the enlightened state.

Happiness as commonly understood is still within the sphere of the personal; it is a stage in Becoming and as such merely the opposite of Suffering. Bliss is the state which results when happiness and suffering, the personal and the impersonal, have been transcended and there is pure Being.

When Zen, or religion for that matter, becomes another 'point of interest' as a subject in itself, i.e. divorced from everyday life, it provides another opportunity for the mind to 'stop', making realization impossible.

Zen is everyday life. If the quality of one's Zen improves, the quality of one's everyday life improves too.

Pure awareness is the complete, if temporary, cessation of the process of identification—that process which creates the illusion of the 'I'.

What does it mean when we designate a man as a liberated being? It means this person is liberated from fear, suffering, in other words, from torturing thoughts. Liberation, being therefore entirely a matter of understanding, can only be approached on the psychological level. Any other approach, such as discipline, exercises, asceticism, etc., must be seen as unlikely to succeed as magic.

The vital energy which in the ordinary person is drained off by the emotions to be converted into some form of action or thought, is in the awakened man conserved and accumulated for the final explosion of satori.

The Void, Emptiness, Let-go, Desirelessness, Nirvana, Kingdom of Heaven, etc., whilst different on the verbal level, are in essence the same experience—viz., that of the fusion of the thinker and his thought.

You want to get rid of the ego, the source of all suffering. . . . Yet how can you get rid of it, this thing which is put together, without knowing it for what it is. Only when you can *consciously* put it together, can you take it apart and so do away with it.

The strange thing about mindfulness is that it comes when least expected. Sometimes when we feel in the mood to give ourselves wholeheartedly to some momentary fascination and be carried away by it—it intervenes and wakes us up from our pretty dream.

'Nature abhors a vacuum'—similarly thought abhors a void. In order not to have to face its empty nature—nothingness—thought invents the thinker to give itself substantiality. Yet the Void is the plenitude of things: everything in phenomenal existence has its roots in that Void.

Any relapse from awareness carries its own reaction, such is the inexorable law of nature: cause-and-effect in events bound by time (the Buddhist law of karma).

Let us live as though every day was our last—we would soon discover the difference between 'being' and 'becoming'.

To many people 'to be religious' is tantamount to being austere, being miserable, in order to be happy in the end (in this life or in the next); to the truly religious man, being religious is being happy, peaceful and joyful, here and now.

People are either escapists or Buddhists in this world.

The spiritual life does not lie away from the everyday life. It *is* the everyday life, unmodified, but with an extra dimension added to it.

Meditation, the cleansing of the mind from recurring torturing thoughts, is as important to mental well being as hygiene is to physical well being.

The truth that unless one is a non-entity there can be no complete happiness must seem hard to swallow in a society that knows the term 'non-entity' only in an unfavourable sense.

BIBLIOGRAPHY

Benoit, Hubert. *The Supreme Doctrine*. London, Routledge & Kegan Paul; New York, Pantheon, 1955.

Blofeld, J., ed. *The Zen Teaching of Huang-Po on the Transmission of Mind*. London, Rider, 1958; New York, British Book Centre, 1959.

Blyth, R. H. *Zen in English Literature and Oriental Classics*. Tokyo, Hokuseido, 1948.

"Ikkyu's Doka," *The Young East,* vol. II, no. 2—vol. III, no. 9. Tokyo, 1952–1954.

Dumoulin, Heinrich. *The Development of Chinese Zen after the Sixth Patriarch,* tr. and ed. Ruth Fuller Sasaki. New York, First Zen Institute, 1953.

Fouéré, René. *Krishnamurti—the Man and his Teaching*. Bombay, Chetana, 1958.

Guirdham, Arthur. *A Theory of Disease*. London, Allen & Unwin, 1957; Hollywood-by-the-Sea, Fla., Transatlantic Arts, 1959.

Isherwood, Christopher, and Swami Prabhavananda. *The Song of God:* Bhagavad Gita. New York, Harper, 1951; London, Phoenix House, 1956.

Krishnamurti, Jiddu. *The First and Last Freedom*. New York, Harper, 1954; London, Victor Gollancz, 1956.

———. Talks. Ojai, California, Krisnamurti Writings Inc.

Murti, T. R. V. *The Central Philosophy of Buddhism,* 2nd ed., London, Allen & Unwin, 1961.

Percheron, Maurice. *Buddha and Buddhism*. London, Longmans; New York, Harper, 1957.

Suzuki, D. T. *Essays in Zen Buddhism,* 3 vols. London, Luzac, 1927, 1933, 1934. Reprinted, Rider, 1949, 1950, 1951; New York, British Book Centre, 1958.

———. *Living by Zen*. London, Rider, 1950.

———. *Manual of Zen Buddhism*. London, Rider, 1956; New York, Grove, 1960.

————. *The Lankavatara Sutra*. London, Routledge & Kegan Paul, 1932. Reprinted 1956.

————. *Zen and Japanese Buddhism*. Tokyo, Japan Travel Bureau; Vermont, Tuttle, 1958.

————. *Zen and Japanese Culture*. London, Routledge & Kegan Paul; New York, Pantheon, 1959.

Watts, Alan W. *The Way of Zen*. London, Thames and Hudson; New York, Pantheon, 1957.

————. *Nature, Man, and Woman*. London, Thames and Hudson; New York, Pantheon, 1958.

Wilson, Colin. *The Outsider*. London, Victor Gollancz; New York, Houghton, 1956.

Wong Mou-lam. *The Sutra of Wei Lang (Hui-neng)*. London, Luzac, 1944.